Wrong Side
of the
Tracks

A Memoir by
Ron McElroy

STILL STANDING®
PUBLISHING

Wrong Side of the Tracks: A Memoir
By Ron McElroy

BIOGRAPHY & AUTOBIOGRAPHY / Personal Memoirs
2. BIOGRAPHY & AUTOBIOGRAPHY / Cultural Heritage
3. BIOGRAPHY & AUTOBIOGRAPHY / General

ISBN: 978-0-9858608-0-6

Cover design by Lewis Agrell
Interior design by Stephanie Martindale

Printed in the United States of America

Still Standing Publishing
www.WrongSideoftheTracksBook.com

For my late father William McElroy, my wonderful mother Tutu, my big brother Bill and big sister Susan, my lovely wife Liz, and three blessed children sons Brett and Cameron, and daughter Lockley. When I think of the life that I have lived, through all of the wild and crazy times as well as times of great enlightenment, I can't imagine changing a single thing. My family, for better or worse, is irreplaceable. Through all of the joys and sorrows, good times and hard times, there is not a better thing in my life than the family I have been blessed with. Thank you, each and every family member, for being my inspiration to do better deeds, write this book and to seek clarity where none seems to exist. Thank you, thank you and thank you!

Contents

Acknowledgements

Many people helped me research and write this book. First of all my mom, Tutu, for being open and forthright about past events, plus my brother Bill, for retracing over old story after old story and for being the original impetus behind this book. I couldn't have done all the research without Donna Foster and Terresa Munoz who helped out tremendously recounting events about my Sister Susan, Denise Brown, for sanctioning her sister's brief mention. Kris McElroy, for encouraging words and historical placement related to this book. Katie Larson, for early emphasis on structure and flow of the story. All of the other friends and family who endured my questions and long follow-up through details and time-frames and places... time after time.

Big thanks to my editor Alan Rinzler for taking this project on after months of me stalking him. Alan brought in a team of professionals including editor and writer Naomi Lucks, copyeditor Leslie Tilley, marketing consultant Stephanie Chandler, jacket designer Lewis Agrell, website designer Steve Coplan, videographer Greg Wilker, and others who worked together to produce this book with skill and good humor.

I must also acknowledge my three kids-Brett, Cameron and Lockley....for being the great kids that they are, freeing up my time to work on projects like this book. Finally, huge thanks to my wife Elisabeth, for sticking it out with me through all the crazy, unpredictable surprises and then for allowing me all the time spent on purging my emotional psyche over the last two years while writing this book.

Ron McElroy, July 2012

Prologue

The phone rang in my room at Sigma Chi, waking me out of a deep, hung-over sleep. The fraternity house at the University of California Santa Barbara was quiet as the dead at this hour of the morning.

It's Sunday, I thought. *Let it ring.*

My girlfriend, Kristen Hodgins, lay close, keeping me warm. But she gave me an elbow in the ribs as the phone kept ringing. Can't be avoided, I guess. I reached over her shoulder, picked up the receiver. It's my mother, calling from L.A.

What crazy ass shit is this going to be?

"Ronnie, come on home. A man just called to tell me your father is out in the desert near Banning, walking backwards and burying his money in the scrub. You got to help me go get him before he hurts himself or does something really crazy! I need your help, right now."

"Where's Billy?"

"Just arrested and on his way back to jail," she says.

Of course, I thought. I didn't have to say it.

Don't get me wrong: my own path had taken some wrong turns. But my big brother, Bill, was a whole other disaster story. Still, he had learned how to completely confound a number of determined cops who'd rather let him out quick than deal with him in one of their holding cells. "Billy can't help," said my mom.

I lay there stroking Kristen's smooth, tan back, smelling the salt coming in off the ocean, feeling the warm Santa Barbara early morning sun already streaming in through the window. The surf was calling.

"What about—"

No, no, and no. Mom's brothers, cousins, and other relatives were either absent, busy, fed up, or otherwise unavailable. Yep, same old family story. No need to say more, really.

"I'll be there," I tell her, already worrying about what I might find out there in the desert. I pulled on my clothes, kissed Kristen good-bye, and took off.

Driving south on 101, I remembered how my mom would always load us three kids into the car after school when she got home from work and head out to go visit my dad at the Long Beach Veterans Hospital psych ward. Like clockwork, he'd either check himself in or get hauled there by the cops for being crazy drunk or just acting nuts.

My mom never acted like visiting him there was strange, or embarrassing. It just was what it was—a family trip to see Dad. We'd always stop at Foster's Freeze, and she'd get me, my brother, and my sister some burgers, fries, and a Coke, a great treat for us. When we got to the hospital, we'd go in with her and see him, unless he was really acting up. Or we'd wait in the hallways, staring at the old guys walking around, bent over their canes, or the younger guys in wheelchairs, just cruising the hallways with nowhere to go.

Sometimes we just waited for her in the car.

Dad was almost always angry, but his really bad mental issues would flare up a couple of times a year for two to four weeks or so. He would just go crazy inside his skin, writhing and squirming and squinting and wincing and then cursing one word after another through clenched teeth at some unfortunate target: *Goddamnmotherfuckin-sonofamotherfuckinnogoodsonofagoddamnmotherfuckin'*— whether it was a real person or just someone in his head who nobody could see but him.

When Billy and I started smoking weed and copying Dad's anger fits, we used to laugh so hard.

Dad's troubles had started up big time when he was in the navy, and he'd seen a navy shrink while he was in the service. They diagnosed him officially with a nervous disorder they politely called "shingles." He was honorably discharged, so he couldn't have caused too much trouble then. But when we were growing up, it was a different story. He would lose it for several days, and then come out of it. I don't think the doctors ever really figured it out.

Anyone could see that his bad craziness had a lot to do with him being a chronic alcoholic. My mom had to drive him to the hospital on three separate occasions when he was "sick," as she called it. Usually, it meant he had downed an entire bottle of something—he loved Seagram's. But anyone could see that his mental wires were crossed way beyond any damage done by alcohol poisoning. Over the years he was also diagnosed with everything from explosive behavior disorder and acute paranoia to manic depression and schizophrenia.

As a kid, I couldn't understand what the problem was. Sometimes I figured it was just the pressure of life. Trying to make ends meet and support his family drove him over the edge. His drinking, or the stress of not drinking those times he tried to stop, got to be too much for him. I thought he'd get it together when things got better, but things never seemed to get better. As I got older, the psychological stuff got worse. Dad got angrier at Billy's antics. Billy got more psycho just because he liked to. And our sweet, shy, beautiful sister Susie left the whole shooting match, running away to join a cult. I couldn't blame her, really, even though it was hard on all of us. She thought she'd found a more understanding family, better than this harsh, unforgiving one that we all grew up in.

Through it all, my mom held her steady Hawaiian course. In the end, I guess, I learned to think like she did about our life: it was what it was.

As it turned out, I never got to the desert that day. The cops and medics had found Dad and taken him to the hospital, where I caught up with my mom about five hours after I got her call. By the time we got there he was in leather straps that anchored his arms and legs tightly to the hospital bed.

For once, Dad was civil, lucid, and calm. He'd come out of his fit and was so sad, I could see it in his eyes, apologetic and remorseful for being in the state he was in. Lying there, strapped to that bed, he was completely helpless. I could see that he understood how let down I was to see him that way. He knew he had really lost it, that he had let us all down.

"I don't know what the hell is going on with me," he said. "I'm sorry. I wish things didn't have to be this way." He shrugged, sad and tearful and quiet, helpless to change anything.

That was the first time I actually cried when I talked to him. I was usually so mad and disappointed that I would just scowl for however long I was forced to listen to him, but this was different.

"It's okay, Dad," I said.

I wished him well, kissed my mom, and left the hospital, holding back my tears. I wished it could have been different too. I turned around and headed north—back to school, back to Kristin, back to the hope of a different life.

But I thought about him all the way.

Chapter One

The first big thing you need to know about me: I have a really big family, and it's often in a lot of trouble. Not a day goes by that I don't hear from one or all of my family members: wife, ex-wife, daughter, sons, mother, brother, sister, uncles, aunties, cousins. . . . And when a family member is in trouble—Billy and my dad being the top two repeat offenders—I can't ignore it or let it go. I need to do something to help. It's sort of like, well, that's my job.

In some ways, my life is a classic immigrant story—learn to fit in, work hard, assimilate, make it big in America, and enjoy the fruits of success. But unlike most American immigrants, who came from Europe or Asia or Latin America, my brother and sister and I were born right here, in Sarasota, Florida. Our dad and his dad were Appalachian hillbillies born and bred. But Mom always held strong to her Hawaiian heritage. In our mom's heart—and in our hearts—we were never Americans, not really. We're Hawaiians, through and through.

So the second big thing you need to know about me: I'm one-quarter pure Hawaiian, and it's the most important part of me.

My family is a kind of rainbow coalition, our own little melting pot of cultures and attitudes: from native Hawaiian to Korean to English-Scottish-German, and more. But the strongest of my many roots starts with my mother's mother Fannie, who was of pure Hawaiian descent, a 100 percent native indigenous Hawaiian, born to a proud, whole-blooded family that maintained considerable land holdings throughout Maui and enjoyed a good life, with all the amenities.

I guess her family figured she'd marry a Hawaiian too, but Fannie was a rebel. She fell deeply in love—a forbidden love, against *kapu,* the ancient Hawaiian code of behavior—with a Korean migrant worker named William Chee Sung Han, who was almost twenty years her senior. When she married the foreigner in spite of her family's protests, they cast her out—off the island. Fannie and William were exiled to Molokai, the most Hawaiian of the Hawaiian islands—a beautiful, sparsely populated volcanic island famous for being a leper colony. Maybe you know it from James Michener's *Hawaii.* It's just a short ferry ride away from Maui, but a million miles away in attitude. Molokai is vehemently undeveloped—you won't find any big tourist resorts there—and kind of spooky. You can feel the ancient Hawaiian nature spirits, rulers of the sun, the rain, the forest, the ocean.

Like my mom says, "Molokai has a lot of spirits."

Fannie lived on Molokai for the rest of her short life, and eventually gave birth to nine live children: seven boys,

William, James, John, Ronald, Harold, Clarence, and Paul; and two girls, my Auntie Ruthie and my mom, Glenna Arlene Han, born on April 21, 1935. Mom always called herself Arlene. But since my son Brett was born, we've all followed his lead and called her Tutu—the Hawaiian word for grandma.

For Tutu, it was a hard life in paradise.

"My days in Molokai was simple, and a struggle," she told me. "My parents called our place 'One-Acre Lot.' We went without stuff—sometimes no shoes to go to school, or shoes were worn out—but we never missed anything. My mother's sisters use to give us hand-me-down clothes."

But pretty soon, this sparse life would start to look pretty good in comparison to what followed: December 7, 1941. That day, the Japanese bombed Pearl Harbor. Soon afterward, Fannie, forty-two, who had already endured a previous stillbirth, died shortly after yet a second stillborn birth. From then on, things for Tutu and her family just went downhill.

One night, a few days after my grandma was buried, the three little ones—my mom, Arlene, her five-year-old brother, Paul, and baby Ruthie, just two years old—were huddled in bed with their dad, looking for comfort. It was dark and dead silent.

"As we lay there," my mom told me, "I heard footsteps coming up the stairs, the doorknobs turning, and a chair moving. . . . At first I thought it was my two older brothers coming home from the movies, but no one came in the house, so my father said that Mom's spirit had come home. We three were so scared.

"Another night, I stood up to turn the lights on, I swear I saw a figure sitting on the chair in the dark. I almost fainted when that happened."

My grandfather must have been haunted too, just like the house. He was never the same after his wife's death. Devastated and despondent, he soon drank himself into a fatal car crash. With both parents dead, the kids had to leave One-Acre Lot. The seven brothers and two sisters would have to create their own love and faith as they became the entire family unit.

"One of my brothers told me that my auntie wanted to adopt us three little ones," Mom told me years later, "but my older brothers said no, because they were afraid they would use us as slaves." At first, the youngest kids had to stay with their next-door neighbor. But after Mom's older brother James got married, he took care of the three little ones.

Mom went to school in Molokai from kindergarten through the seventh grade, and spent some of her time then and later working in the pineapple fields. In those days, thousands of acres of Molokai were devoted to commercial pineapple cultivation.

"I tell you, it is not an easy job!" she once said. "You have to cover yourself from head to toe—goggles, a big hat, and your clothes had to be denim, long sleeves, so that the pineapple stickers don't stab you."

When she was thirteen, her oldest brother, Bill, got married and took Arlene, Paul, and Ruthie to live with him in Honolulu. Bill was a World War II veteran who was awarded a Purple Heart when he was injured at Normandy Beach. He put the whole family in veteran's housing. With no car, the kids walked to school about a mile through the sugar cane fields. After a few years, the little family left the veteran's housing and rented a small house in Kaimuki, near Diamond Head.

My Mom is a killer combo—tiny, beautiful, and smart—and a hard worker determined to take care of herself and her family no matter what. She has earned her own way pretty much her entire life. By 1953 she had graduated from high school and was hard at work in the Libby's pineapple cannery in Honolulu, earning her own money. She saved up enough to fulfill her dream to visit the mainland. So in August of that year she went to live with her brother Ron and his wife and baby in navy housing in San Diego, California, where she signed up to attend junior college. Eventually, she moved to Los Angeles, worked as a clerk at an insurance company, met a tall, good-looking guy named Bill McElroy, got pregnant with my brother, chased Bill to Florida where, improbably, he was an art student, studying on the G.I. Bill, but with periodic visits to the VA psych ward for mental problems. They finally married and had two more kids, my big sister and me, the youngest.

Mom was sure to give all her kids both regular American names but also

Hawaiian names. My brother Bill's name was Keola, my sister Susan was Leelani, and I was Hale, after my uncle Ron, pronounced Hah-Lee, two syllables.

Dad never finished art school, and we all moved back to L.A.

But that's another story. What I really want to talk about first is Hawaii.

∾

I first visited the Hawaiian Islands with my mom and my brother and sister in 1965, when I was seven years old. I wasn't used to flying, and the descent into the Honolulu airport had me a little worried. But as the plane taxied down the runway I forgot my apprehension fast. We walked out onto a stairway that was rolled right up to the plane and took us down onto the tarmac. The air was so tropical and fresh smelling, warm and moist, and the sky was a magnificent blue, so much bluer than I ever remember our smoggy sky back in California. But that was only the beginning.

Each passenger who got off the plane was greeted personally by two beautiful Polynesian women. And they were wearing hula skirts! I reached the bottom of the stairway and a Hawaiian goddess smiled down at me with the most exotic pair of brown eyes. She leaned in closer and kissed me gently on the cheek as she put a lei over my head and around my neck. The fragrance of the fresh flowers, the closeness of her soft skin on mine, and the lasting red imprint of her kiss are still with me. Then another Hawaiian goddess smiled and handed me a small cup of pineapple juice. Our greeters were all smiles and very gracious, as if this was a genuine experience not only for us, but for them as well.

Wow, I thought. *This Hawaii is really great.*

There was something new to see everywhere. I was fascinated by the airport, where—for some puzzling reason—old burnt-out wreckage of jet planes lined the runway. And as we drove toward Waikiki to my Uncle Paul's house, I couldn't help but notice all the new high-rise buildings going up. It seemed like hundreds, surrounded by huge cranes. A multitude of new condos, hotels, and apartments were blooming out of the wet tropical landscape. I'd seen buildings before, but these were somehow different—vibrant, active. An optimistic buzz poured into everything that the sunshine touched. The tall swaying coconut trees waved in the trade winds, palm fronds shimmering as they twisted and turned. *Like cheerleaders,* I thought, urging the day on with their green pom-poms. I was so excited by all the Waikiki hustle-bustle that I could barely sit still.

When we reached my Uncle Paul's house in a quiet little neighborhood just outside of the city, things began to calm down a bit. His wife, my Auntie Sissy, was so friendly, all smiles. I soon realized that it wasn't just the greeters at the airport—every greeting from a female relative or friend included a kiss on the cheek, so different than what I was used to. Right away, I was struck by how much Hawaiians touched each other just in the course of a normal interaction. And the words *auntie, uncle, brah* (meaning brother) and *cousin* almost always accompanied a greeting. I knew that everybody I met couldn't possibly be related to me—although there were a lot of those—but Hawaiians just used these warm terms with anyone they considered family, like good friends.

I felt right at home, no question. And we were staying for two weeks!

◇

We had a lot of Sunday school and church while growing up in L.A. It was a regular thing for my mom and the three of us kids, but I don't ever remember Dad coming with us to church. I thought Sunday school was fun, like play time. But the sermon's were boring and I couldn't wait to get out. So when Mom started off our trip to Hawaii by taking us to be baptized at her brother Bill's church, I was expecting more of the same. I was so wrong.

At that time Jesus Coming Soon was a small church in Honolulu, where my uncle, Pastor Bill, had built up quite a respectable fellowship of god-fearing patrons over the years. Jesus Coming Soon was Hawaiian holy-rolling gospel at its finest, bringing down the house. I can see it like it was yesterday: me and Susie and Billy are front and center, standing side by side wearing white, full-length robes over our bathing suits, looking like startled little mice waiting to be submerged into God's good graces. Whew!

I was awestruck, fascinated, and petrified at being in front of the entire congregation—so many people, all of them carrying on loud and enthusiastically, as if it was just a grand old thing to be alive and well. Not used to being the center of attention, especially to a large strange crowd, and a loud one at that, I was a bit scared—but just a little bit, because I know that these people were considered family by all of my relatives. That made it a little easier to find comfort in this awkward situation.

The church itself, with its huge vaulted ceilings, seemed to tower over us. The walls were partially clad with volcanic stone, the floors covered in red carpeting, and a massive cross with Jesus nailed to it looked over everyone. The waiting seemed to go on and on.

Then, for no reason I could tell, there was a break in the loud singing. My cousin, Billy Han Junior (yes, there are a lot of Bills in my family), poked his head around the corner off to the side of the stage.

"Okay, you guys ready?"

He's pretty enthusiastic. We all nod slowly.

Billy Junior waves us to come forward, so we follow him out in a line to the stage. We're standing above and behind this large volcanic rock wall that has a glass fronted pool at least eight feet across, with steps leading down into it. You can see everything in the pool, like something at Marine World. There's enough room for a small basketball team in there! Obviously, we're not the first to be baptized at Jesus Coming Soon, nor will we be the last. But we were walking down those steps whether we wanted to or not.

Mom told me then, and assures me to this day, that the only reason she is alive is because her Mom, Fannie, took her to the Jesus Coming Soon church in Molokai a couple of days after she was born—a blue baby, deprived of oxygen at birth—and had her baptized. And now it seemed that Mom's brother, Pastor Bill, also placed significant importance in being baptized. Come to think of it, this was probably my mom's primary objective in getting all of us kids back to Hawaii at an early age: so she could baptize us at the Jesus Coming Soon church and protect us forever and ever.

So there we were, finally, standing in waist-deep water, looking out into the congregation. They were all staring back at us. My Uncle Bill was in the tank with us quoting scripture, dressed in a white robe like ours, holding his big Bible with one hand and gesturing with the other.

"May god bless these children and keep them safe through temptation and ill will. . . . " And on and on and on. I tried not to look at the congregation. I tried to keep the fright from surging back, but it was hard.

Every once in a while, the thought that I was related to this rock star of a minister running this whole huge church would creep in to give me a brief secure feeling. It was really a beautiful thing for someone like my Uncle Bill to spend all this time and effort in front of his entire congregation for us, asking for all of those prayers to be directed strictly for our protection and well-being.

Then, one kid at a time, he started. For some reason I was first, so I had no idea what I was in for. Uncle Bill put one hand on my forehead, the other on my shoulder. He said a deep, deliberate last rites of blessing and forcefully dunked me into the pool. He held me down for a few seconds, fully submerged, and I wondered how long I could hold my breath.

One, two, three . . . Then he brought me back upright forcefully in the name of the Lord and the Holy Ghost. *Whew!*

I was glad that I was done first. After a few more prayers and a few loud hymns by the raucous congregation we were all three of us—Billy, Susie, and me—baptized, blessed by God, and protected from life's many travesties, with which mom and her brothers were all too familiar.

We stayed with Uncle Pastor Bill and family for the next couple of days. Running around their sprawling property made me feel so connected to Hawaii. Mom had us staying with each of our uncles for a couple of days each. The uncles fought over their share of time with her, so she had to be mindful about giving each of them equal shares of visiting.

What a great time that was, staying with each of the families, playing, and getting to know each set of our cousins—cousins I would grow up to be tight with from then on. I could see that my mom felt good about it all, but it's only been recently that I learned that simple things I'd always taken for granted, or had not given more than an idle thought to as a kid, turned out to be of utmost importance to her. She truly felt one of her fundamental tasks was to save every penny she got her hands on to get her kids back to Jesus Coming Soon, so we could receive our cloak of invisible armor against all the evils that life would surely impose on each one of us.

Like a salmon's going back upstream to spawn, her long journey has paid off, at least for me. The acceptance I felt from my mom's family, and the deep understanding of Hawaii I practically inhaled from them, would change me forever. The *kapu* concept of right and wrong, good versus evil, was impressed upon my young brain very early. It pulled me back from the brink of oblivion many times. Maybe it was guilt about what these people who prayed and sang for me might think, but thoughts of them have stopped me many times from going entirely over the edge. Pretty close, but not entirely over the edge.

My second baptism on that trip came by way of my Uncle Paul, because he taught me to surf. I went with Uncle Paul and my cousins to the clear warm water at Ewa Beach. The ocean surrounds everything in Hawaii—you can't escape the sound of the waves, the salty air, the endless blue and green stretching off forever. It's a beautiful sight, and I never get tired of it. But riding those waves for the first time was something else entirely.

Today's surfers like short boards, but in those days twelve-foot-long boards were standard—so there was plenty of room for a small kid to sit up front with the regular surfer behind. Uncle Paul was such the proficient waterman—he could surf, spearfish, bodysurf, swim, or paddle long distances. When he put me on his board, kneeled behind me, and started paddling out over the smaller inside waves, the rhythm of his stroke was like a motor, the digging motion deliberate and precise. And even with my dead weight on the front of the board, he never got off balance. The whole experience was more than I could imagine, in every way.

So far in my brief life, I had grown up with virtually no interaction with my father, especially not anything to do with sports or fun. So being way out in the ocean with a male authority figure who was laughing and encouraging me? It was surreal. And then, before I knew what was happening, Uncle Paul paddled us right into a wave and coached me upright:

"Stand up, shift your feet, hold your hands out for balance, shoot your stance farther apart, . . ." It seemed easy, but the water was moving by so fast! Still, I found my balance and never looked back. Crouched, with my arms extended . . . I could have done that over and over all day long. What a day.

Uncle Paul took me to a local surf shop and bought me my first real pair of surf trunks: Hang Ten mustard colored shorts with two footprints, the Hang Ten logo, at the bottom of the right leg. It even had a Velcro fly—a big deal at the time, especially for a kid. I was hooked on surfing from that day forward. Forever after, I would beg, borrow, steal, or hitchhike to go surfing. It really hooked me, for life.

≈

Just as Mom had lost no time making sure that her wayward children were baptized into the evangelical Christianity that was popular with so many Hawaiians, she made sure we were equally immersed in the deeper, more pervasive Hawaiian spirituality—which despite nearly 200 years of oppression, has never been driven from the island or the consciousness of real Hawaiians. She did it by bringing us back to where it had all started with her, to Hoʻolehua in Molokai, to visit all the many relatives we had on that island.

Chapter Two

Molokai was another world—old-school Hawaii, with all its natural beauty. Not a single paved road existed on the island when I went there the first time, but I could see right away why my mom loved Molokai so much. Hoʻolehua was nothing short of magnificent.

Rural as it gets, Hoʻolehua was a Hawaiian Homelands agricultural homestead—land given back to the Hawaiians whose land it had been in the first place. The Hawaiian Homelands was a worthy idea with a typically bureaucratic method behind it.

It starts out simply: If you are at least 50 percent Hawaiian by blood, then you qualify to put your name on a list to receive a Hawaiian Homelands Property. The property can be in the form of agricultural land (usually in the two- to ten-acre range), a lot designated for a residential dwelling, or a home in which you would have to at least qualify to make payments on the financed improvements on the land. Each island has a program, and as new areas are designated, notifications go out in chronological order. Sounds easy, right?

Later in life, just listening to Tutu talk about her time waiting for her Maui property made it seem like a pretty long, arduous endeavor. I think Tutu was on the list for maybe ten years, and the only reason she was able to get a chance at the house she later retired to was because not that many Hawaiians in line before her could qualify to take out a mortgage on a loan amount of $120,000 to $150,000. I helped guide her through the acceptance part of the process, qualifying and backing her on the finance portion of the mortgage. It was something else.

Her name was put into a pool of about a hundred other qualified buyers who all together pretty much filled the small gymnasium. A bucket was passed around for the qualifiers to pick a number out of. Whatever number you got put you in line to be able to choose the lot, and one of four styles of house to be constructed on that lot. If you ended up with a lot not to your liking and you found another Hawaiian in the same situation, you could trade lots. Of course, because it was Hawaii, the whole process was like a big luau picnic. No stress or anguish because you didn't get the right lot. Everyone was just happy and even glad to see other people getting a good lot and house.

Of course, later on it can go downhill fast. When you die you can pass the property along to your children or next of kin, even if they are not the required 50 percent Hawaiian by blood. That's good. But if the receiving offspring are married to non-Hawaiians, making their offspring even *less* Hawaiian, it can make for a pretty convoluted group of owners! And selling the property gets pretty crazy. There might eventually be twenty, thirty, even forty separate owners, and no one can come to a consensus on what to do with the property. Sometimes Hawaiian Homelands property is just abandoned because resolving all the difficulties surrounding its use is just too much trouble.

∽

But I didn't know any of this when I was seven and seeing Molokai for the first time. All I saw was beauty and no city. Green pineapple fields lined with deep red dirt roads dominated the rolling landscape. Everything was permanently stained with red dirt—I mean everything, even everyone's feet, because everyone went barefoot. No one wore shoes. The town itself looked, to me at least, like something out of an old western.

My Auntie Kalama and Uncle Jimmy's house, where we were staying, was about as different from my house as I could imagine. Not that our place in L.A. was any great thing, but this was one rudimentary shelter. Nothing glamorous about it. The wooden floor felt solid under foot, yet worn, and discolored by the stain of red dirt. The walls were all single-wall construction—as opposed to walls I was used to, where the wires were installed with the insulation between inside and outside walls. Here, the electrical wires were visible, secured to the wall or ceiling. A single, bare light bulb hung from the center of the small family room, illuminating an old tattered couch, a single simple end table, and that was it.

The kitchen, directly off the family room, had a freestanding stove and sink, the type I was used to seeing in a laundry room. The painted wooden walls, light switch boxes, and door frames all showed years of continual use.

Even the light switch itself was worn to an irregular shape and color. I noticed the deep groove in the right corner edge of the kitchen sink, where Kalama always cleaned her long knife blade after filleting a fish or chopping a pineapple. Years of Jimmy coming home from a long day in the fields, and kids running in and out with dirty hands, had stained the handle and opening edge of the front door a deep red. The lacy curtains blowing out from the windows had once been white, but they were tinted red too. The two bedrooms off the main room had a bed in each one, and that was it. Everyone shared. I looked around for where we would sleep, and found out it would be with Billy and Susie on a makeshift bed on the family room floor. And that's really where my introduction to religion Hawaiian style began.

Every night when we went to sleep, Auntie Kalama would sprinkle salt over us while murmuring a prayer. I never heard the entire prayer, but it definitely had to do with asking for protection through the night.

Why is she so concerned about protecting us, I wondered, *and from what?*

I started thinking about all the stories I'd been hearing since we got here. "Oh Ronnie," someone would say, "you no can go that way, brah, no. This is *kapu*. If you cross the path, brah, you going get big trouble." And someone else would chime in, "Oh, yeah, brah, the *menehunes* come in the night and take your stuff or ruin your stuff. No kidding, brah!" And they were not kidding. Those stories weren't just for amusement, like I'd been thinking.

These stories and warnings didn't bother me during the day. But in the pitch dark, with the constant moaning wind and the blowing red lace curtains—and all preceded by the hour-long prayer and salt-sprinkling ritual—I started having trouble sleeping. Lying there on the floor, every thump sounded like a ghostly footstep, every wind-driven howl seemed like a faraway scream or sorrowful moan. The whole place was alive with discontent. I remember lying awake all night listening to what I was sure was a woman's plea for help to find her lost babies.

Whoooo, scary!

My Auntie Kalama's precautions, like the salt ritual, were deliberate and regular, just like brushing your teeth. And she was by no means a special case. Hawaiians by nature are very superstitious, particularly when it comes to respecting the power of nature. If you take too much from the land or the sea, then the land and the sea will take it back—directly, like through a drought that leaves your starved or fish that don't want to get caught. Bad luck is not considered to be random; it's purposeful retribution for your disrespect to your elders, your ancestors, and worst of all to the provider of all that is good and whole, Mother Earth.

This was a self-monitoring system that must have worked well to teach kids to behave even when the teachers or parents weren't around. If you know that your behavior is always under scrutiny—not just by Santa around Christmas, but by the earth and wind and water twenty-four hours a day—you're always going to be wary of acting badly. In a way, it's like saying God is always watching you, waiting for you to make a mistake and be sent to hell. Maybe that's why the Hawaiian population has assimilated so well into some fundamental forms of Christianity.

The stories of old warrior spirits, *menehunes*—little leprechaun-type people who were said to live in the forest—or the dire consequences of going against *kapu,* were abundant and frequently shared with us kids, whether we wanted to hear them or not. The way the elders told the stories, they were fact—not some random fairytales from the past. Spirits were everywhere. I had heard some of these stories from my mother in the past, but that was in L.A. There was something different about hearing them again here, in Molokai, where thousands of warriors were rumored to have perished in the valley directly behind my Auntie Kalama's house.

So it's not surprising that our early morning visit to my grandparents' gravesite was also like something out of a horror movie for us little kids. The tombstones were large carved granite stones with old wilted flowers all around them, shrouded in fog. All I could think about were my mom's stories about how all the valleys, *like the one we were in right now,* were populated with *menehunes* and haunted by the spirits of slaughtered warriors. I was always looking over my shoulder. Scary as heck!

My mom told and retold us stories that haunted me throughout my childhood and even into early adulthood. I used to wonder if her beliefs and superstitions were the result of being orphaned at an early age and having to figure out a lot of things for herself, or if they were standard procedure for her culture. But now the answer was clear: losing her mom when she was just a little kid, and then having her dad die a few years later—all that was certainly traumatic. But I could see even at the age of seven how accepted and ingrained her superstition was in Hawaiian culture.

In Hawaii, it's real.

$\sim$

For thousands of years, Molokai must truly have been paradise, at least in those moments when warriors weren't clashing and spirits weren't doing their mischief. Molokai was considered to be an ancient center of wisdom and spirituality, and the birthplace of the hula—which was not conceived as a dance to entertain tourists but as a religious experience.

But that was a long time ago. Hawaii and its culture were changed, driven down, and nearly lost with the continued immigrations of non-Hawaiian outsiders to Hawaii: Chinese, Japanese, Koreans, Filipinos, and then Europeans—Portuguese, Spanish, English—and finally, the Americans.

The American takeover of the Hawaiian Islands has been steady. The illegal annexation of the islands by the United States in 1898 is commonly referred to as the first major instance of American imperialism. Assimilation of the native Hawaiians, like my family, transformed a warrior culture into an underclass, similar to what happened to Native Americans on the mainland. The colonialists have used generations of native Hawaiians to work the fields and maintain the uniquely attractive Hawaiian attributes necessary to draw tourists to visit the sprawling new resorts. Both before and after statehood for Hawaii, the people who actually govern Hawaii have always put American financial and military interests above those of the indigenous people who still live on the islands.

In the beginning, most Hawaiians believed they needed nothing from the outsiders. But they were land rich and cash poor, so as the outsiders established a stronger foothold, and took over more and more of the land, Hawaiians eventually realized that if they wanted to survive at all they had no choice but to work for money. Agriculture—mostly sugar and pineapples—became huge money-making enterprises for Europeans and employment opportunities for Hawaiians. By 1965, when I first visited the islands, just about all of Molokai's volcanic landscape was deep green pineapple fields crisscrossed with red roads for as far as you could see. It was beautiful, but it was beauty driven by harsh necessity, commerce, and the need to survive.

All the families seemed to exist off of working the pineapple fields, farming, or fishing. That's all there was on the island. Whole families worked the fields. All the local kids had worked on the pineapple fields at one time or another while growing up. I had been fascinated by the bottoms of my mom's feet, which I would stare at while she was lying on the couch watching TV; the entire sole was one big callus. Now I began to understand why. When Mom was a child, they picked pineapples all day long in the Dole fields.

Those fields closed on Molokai in 1985, but today, just like other Americans, Hawaiians must work to make money to pay for new imported things—and when you live on an island in the middle of the ocean, most things come from somewhere else. There are some benefits of being incorporated into the United States: security, better health standards, some employment opportunities. But you can't simply ignore what has happened to the original Hawaiian people.

The tragic history of the Hawaiian Islands is not too different than that of a lot of other conquered lands in earlier centuries: indigenous population decimated by foreign diseases, lands confiscated because they were strategic militarily (think Pearl Harbor) or agriculturally significant (think pineapples and sugar cane), and, finally and inevitably, colonization.

On Molokai, where 40 percent of the population—about eight thousand people—is native Hawaiian, resistance is still strong and vocal. Everybody knows that Molokai is where the real Hawaiians live, the vigilante resisters, the last holdouts who refuse to play along with the conquerors. My mom was born into the heartland of a grassroots sovereignty movement where the angry young men muttered against the *haole,* the white colonialists, the caucasian Europeans who kept doing their best to stamp them out of existence.

Further tragedy came with the struggle to adjust to new ways and the conflict that created with traditional values. The long-term difficulties caused by assimilation are both cultural and physical. Cultural conflicts result in strained family relations and divisive estate battles, when family members don't accept the idea of sharing of Hawaiian properties with siblings who have married non-Hawaiian spouses. Physical problems are plenty. Diabetes is a plague. Amputations and early death from diabetes are fairly common health risks for Hawaiians. And now widespread addiction to crystal meth and other drugs pose significant risks, especially for young people but also for older folks.

The people of Molokai are sometimes stigmatized as lazy or stubborn because they don't allow new development on the island. One big reason is that the people control the rights to the water, though there have been attempts—so far unsuccessful—to strip them of these rights. Recently, the only big resort on the island, Molokai Ranch, was forced to close for lack of water access. So these sovereign Hawaiians are willing to sacrifice the tourist business jobs to maintain a small piece of the Hawaiian culture.

My mom taught me that being Hawaiian should never be anything but pride, not shame, and on Molokai, this spirit is alive and well.

∼

The core of traditional Hawaii—the one thing that remains strong and vibrant—is the feeling of family.

In honor of our visit, Mom's family threw a huge luau-style feast. Aunties, uncles, cousins, *tutus, braddas,* and *titas* (brothers and sisters). Hundreds of Hawaiian men, women, and children who were somehow related to us just seemed to appear from everywhere, from all directions, emerging from the bushes and the side roads. I met so many new aunties, uncles, and cousins that it was absolutely impossible to keep track of who belonged to which immediate family, let alone attempt to memorize their names. Kealoha, Kalani, Kamakea . . . these were just a few of the K names from one family! And every one of them was carrying more food. It was a typical Hawaiian show of respect and gratitude, but I'd never seen anything like it in my life.

We had every kind of Hawaiian dish you've ever heard of—and many that I hadn't until that trip.

"Black dog" was the strangest one—a black soup-type dish made out of pig's blood. I passed on that one, but the rest was pretty great. Poi, of course, was plentiful—the heavy, pasty pudding made from taro root is a traditional Hawaiian food. Then there was *lomi lomi,* salmon cubes mixed with onions and tomatoes; *limo,* a kind of seaweed; octopus that someone had speared and cut into bite-sized pieces; *opihi,* a salted crustacean picked from rocks where waves crash; jerky made from a deer someone had shot; macadamia nuts; assorted fruits—bananas, papayas, guava, breadfruit, mangos—not to mention the ubiquitous American-type dishes like potato salad, macaroni salad, bread, noodles, and sticky white rice that you always see at luaus.

My uncles had gone hunting for wild boar, so the luau's main course was succulent *kalua* pig. The whole process of cooking it was unlike any barbecue I'd ever imagined. The day before the luau, the men dug a big pit called an *imo* and filled it volcanic rock—which, on a volcanic island, is pretty easy to come by. They built a fire to heat up the rock and got it good and hot for a few hours. Meantime, they dressed the pig and wrapped it in banana leaves and *ti* leaves, and lowered it down. Then they covered it and let cook for hours. You've never had anything as good as this! And as if that wasn't enough, they made some of it into *lau lau.* They took the cooked pork and mixed it up with butterfish, fat, and taro, wrapped it up in *ti* leaves, and steamed the grapefruit-sized balls of food in a pressure cooker. Incredible taste! Unforgettable.

But the luau was about more than the food; it reinforced and strengthened the warm family feelings that had already been stirred up by our trip to Hawaii. Tutu made sure that we understand where she—and we—came from.

On that first visit she showed us all the places of her childhood: where she grew up, where she went to school and how she got there, where her parents died and where they were buried. She told crazy stories about her brothers and how they liked to hunt, going off for a couple of days into the mountains and returning with wild boar or deer for the family to eat. Mom told one story about her younger brother, Paul—the one who taught me how to surf, and my favorite uncle after Clarence—that resonated for me.

Paul was always in trouble. One day, Mom said, he thought it would be funny to light the field behind the airport on fire and pee it out. Well, eventually he ran out of pee and the fire got out of hand and burnt down the one tiny sugar plantation–style building that was the airport. He got in big trouble for that. The older brothers would usually take care of him through thick or thin, but they had no tolerance for behavior of this sort. He got smacked around a fair amount, my mom said.

I could see my own brother, Billy, doing something along those lines. I grinned a lot hearing about Paul as a young guy who got in trouble.

But hold on. We just touched on something important. That's the third big thing you should know about me: my big brother, Billy.

～

Billy is my elder brother by two-and-a-half years. We grew up under the same roof, were raised by the same parents, went to the same schools and churches—heck, we were even baptized together on that trip at the Jesus Coming Soon Church. But the paths we chose to walk turned out to be quite different.

Don't get me wrong—I'm no perfect role model. But early on, Bill jumped on Mr. Toad's Wild Ride for a few spins and liked it so much he never got off. Whether his go-for-broke behavior is genetic or a relentless series of poor judgments and missteps, his adventures and misadventures—combined with my obsessive need to be his caretaker—have brought our paths to a perfect made-for-TV Dr. Phil intersection many, many times.

Billy was the oldest, Susie came next, and I was the baby. We grew up in less than ideal circumstances, literally on the wrong side of the tracks—in fact the tracks were my playground, running right through our neighborhood in Buena Park. You've probably already figured out that our family's economic and psychological circumstances were far from the American Dream of *Ozzie and Harriet*–style apple pie. Dad was mentally unstable and a raging alcoholic—he practically had it stamped on his forehead like a giant sign advertising a Going Out of Business Sale. Like all alcoholics, he was unpredictable.

But one thing never varied: he always treated me and Susie a lot better than he did my big brother. My father treated Billy with absolute disdain. Even when I was only four or five years old I could always see the difference, and I wondered why.

Many years later, I learned that Billy had been a mistake—the Big Mistake that caused my pregnant mom to chase my father down from Los Angeles to a VA psych ward in the beautiful state of Florida, where my grandpa, William Luther McElroy (surely drunk off his ass himself), convinced my dad, the part-time art student, that marrying his pregnant girlfriend was the right thing to do. Actually, I think they got married right then and there at the hospital. Happy young couple, off to a great start.

There are so many places to dig for answers in our family history that you'd hit China three times before you found a fraction of the information needed to make some sense of it all. My dad was discharged from the navy and tossed in the loony bin. He lost his mother, lost his home, his own father was too drunk to care—and now throw an unexpected child and shotgun marriage in for good measure—I guess I can understand the reasons for my dad's emotional problems and the weight of responsibility it put on their firstborn.

Maybe it was my mom's Hawaiian sense of family, but our parents stayed together through it all. She married a guy right there in the psych ward, so I guess she knew what she was getting into. Still, these two people from equally decimated family units found each other and struck out into life together, attempting to hold on to the shreds of security and stability that had been so quickly snatched from them both at such an early age.

I've heard the stories, and I've spent a lot of time looking at the old, crumpled, yellowed photos. I look into their eyes, frozen in time, and see piercing stares that speak silently of obligation, their lives mired in unfortunate circumstances and their grief compounded by more unfortunate circumstances, seeking comfort in each other like a reflection in a mirror. I guess it's unfair to expect the outcome to turn out much better than it did.

With no stable models in their own lives to emulate, their parenting skills were based on trial and error. Mom had very strong old-school Hawaiian values and beliefs, both spiritual and practical. She always saw the bright side and still does, living her life with the Hawaiian attitude towards everything, never bitter or unhappy. She just did what she had to.

As the first child, Billy undoubtedly received the brunt of their confused emotional assaults parading as parental guidance. For my brother, determining right from wrong must have been no less difficult than tying your shoes with one hand behind your back—far easier to walk around with unlaced shoes. Maybe they got better at it as they went along, or maybe I was just an easier kid to raise. But by the time I came along a couple of years later after Bill and Susie, our parents seemed more able to give me kindness and affection. Even Dad.

That difference in attitude on my father's part towards his two sons made no difference to me or how I felt about Billy. I looked up to my charming, athletic, brave, rebellious, and reckless brother as my hero. I watched him get in trouble—really bad trouble—at home, in the neighborhood, in school, with the cops. I often had to cover for him, but I wanted to be just like him. Fortunately for me, I wasn't.

Blessed with fortune is the only way to describe my life. It's like a big jigsaw puzzle, and I'm constantly looking for the right pieces to plug into the right spaces. They always seem to be there if I just look hard enough.

Billy, on the other hand, never had the attention span required to locate the right pieces, let alone match them with anything. He'd rather set the puzzle on fire and leave everyone else to salvage the burnt pieces.

Chapter Three

Coming back home from Hawaii after spending the summer there in 1965 was a dose of culture shock— no waving palm trees, no warm extended family, no island spirits watching my every move. Worse, Buena Park is landlocked, home to Knott's Berry Farm, and next door to Anaheim and Disneyland—but it was no theme park.

Hearing my parents arguing, Dad constantly ragging on Billy, I was walking on eggshells all the time so my dad didn't explode—or worse, make me to stay inside with him on a sunny day to watch *The Battle of Midway* on TV for the fifth time for no reason, instead of playing ball in the street with my friends. It was abusive and volatile, and it took a toll on me emotionally as I got older. But it all seemed normal to me at the time.

I hung out with all the other neighborhood kids, and there were a bunch of them. We played baseball and foot-ball on our street; there were definitely no soccer moms in our neighborhood. Most of us kids were on our own, which was fine with us. We wandered off to nearby fields and built makeshift forts and tree houses whenever we wanted. No one ever worried about child abduction or molestation back then, so we just roamed around. Every once in a while one of us would encounter a creepy freak, but it never amounted to anything.

The train trestle behind our housing tract was our best playground. We'd dare each other to climb up high under the trestle, to see if you could handle it when the train passed over. It would just shake your brains out. The best times were after a big rain, when the water would be flowing underneath the trestle like a river. We'd tie a garden hose to the top center support beam and swing from one side to the other on that stretchy hose. The point was to see who could get the biggest swing closest to the water without hitting the surface and having to be reeled in somehow. It was crazy fun.

∼

By junior high school I was a big guy, and naturally talented at sports. I played baseball and football, and made most valuable player and all-stars every year. But at the same time, by the seventh grade I had started drinking and smoking weed.

One night I came home wasted, my eyes all red—a dead giveaway. Mom had seen this before, and she didn't want me following in Billy's footsteps. So she responded from her gut: she started throwing cans of peaches and soup, winging them at me across the kitchen.

"I know you were with your brother, weren't you? It's his fault, isn't it?" She would never accept that my bad behavior was my fault.

I just ducked the cans and kept on doing what I was doing. Billy got into so many bad things that whatever I did was a drop in the bucket by comparison.

One day after school, I arrived home and was excited to see that all my fellow street gamers were organizing a game of over-the-line. All of us kids were always up for a good game of baseball, football, skating, bike ramps—whatever we came up with from one day to the next.

"Hey, you guys look pretty weak, I should be on your team."

"Yeah, makes sense."

"We'll take Bobby's brother Tommy to keep it even."

"All right, cool."

Tommy was the younger brother of a good friend of mine who lived across the street. He was a good kid, just not terribly gifted when it came to sports.

"Come on, you moron, hit the ball!"

All of us kids pretty much had grown up with each other since we were toddlers, so there were no qualms about dishing each other healthy doses of grief whenever possible.

"Batter, batter, you suck, batter."

Just then I see my mom driving up in her blue-green Ford Galaxy, shooting me a glance I translate instantly: *Get your butt over here, now!* Ahhh, just got going, too.

She yells out the window, "Ronnie, go get your sister Susie, and come with me in the car. We need to find your brother." She just knew he was out there geting in trouble, and this was the only way she could think of to stop him.

"Oh, great, Mom. You know we're not going to find him. And if we do, what then?"

"I'll make him come home if I have to pull him by his ear, that's what!" And she drove off home to change out of her work clothes.

All right, I have to miss the street game, but whatever. I ran in the house, found Susie in her room, and told her she had to get in the car.

"Mom says *now!*"

We could both hear Mom hustling around, changing out of her dressy work clothes, scanning the house, impatient to leave.

Susie came along slowly, reluctantly, and clearly not happy about it. But Susie never argued or complained. That's just the way she was with everything back then: compliant. My sister was a genuine beauty, inside and out. She and I knew each other better than anyone else. She could tell when I was upset or pissed off, but where I tended to let it all out—on the field, or in fights, or goofing around at the edge of danger—she kept it all inside. But even though she was shy and quiet, she had lots of friends. Not only was she a cheerleader in junior high, she also played girls softball and was pretty good, getting nominated to the all-star team regularly. At this moment she probably just wanted to be left alone to do her homework, but she followed me out quietly.

So we got in the back in the car, off with Mom on another family re-bonding experience. I looked at my fellow over-the-liners, all laughing and pointing at me for having to leave the game, and gave them the bird.

~

I was no stranger to these family search-and-rescue missions. Sometimes it was my dad we were dragging home.

He was usually marooned at one of the many bars in the neighborhood, rehydrating with the rest of the after-work drinkers. Always a treat to find his unmistakable dirty, bright orange, early model Ford pickup. We kids would get to sit and watch my four-foot-eleven Mom try to yank my six-foot-one angry Dad away from his ice-cold brew and inebriated cronies.

Mom is and always has been fighter for what she wants. Sometimes I question exactly why she wanted Dad, but that's all water under the bridge by now.

After they got married in the VA hospital, Dad eventually wound up attending the Ringling School of Art in Sarasota and working part time at several jobs to support the family. He could draw pretty well, and had done portraits of his friends in the navy to make extra money. He intended to become a commercial artist, I guess, but that didn't work out. Billy was born in 1955, Susie came along in 1957, and I followed one year later, in 1958. By that time, Mom had had it with Florida and missed her family.

In 1959, with Dad only a few months away from graduation, Mom decided to take us kids and move back to California to live with her brother Clarence. Every Monday morning, Dad would send her a check. Then one day he just showed up.

"One morning there was a knock on the door, and there was your dad," she told me. "He missed us so much that he packed the car with all our belongings and drove all the way to California." It sounds romantic, the way she tells it.

So Dad didn't finish art school, and never did become a commercial artist. But Mom always finished what she started, and then some. She had started out as a shipping clerk when she first started working for North American Aviation. She only took off work for a few years when we were little, at my dad's request. But Dad just couldn't cut it as a full-time breadwinner. He had an asphalt paving business the whole time we were growing up, but when he was drinking he wasn't working, so his company never amounted to much in those days.

So Mom got her job back and went back to work with a vengeance. She made sure the mortgage was paid, the kids had food, and the lights stayed on. She was smart, focused, and a great worker, so she was promoted to secretary and then administrative assistant to a team of engineers. She worked at North American and a few other incarnations of the same company—thirty-four years in total.

Meanwhile Dad was working just enough to go out and drink. My dad made money and lost it all over the years of his rocky life, but Mom left her job with a great pension and Social Security to carry her through the rest of her years.

My mom's fight to keep the family together was nothing short of heroic, although no one really wanted it to stay together except for her, God bless her.

Sometimes Billy just seemed to need to run away, an act he'd been perfecting since the ripe old age of ten or eleven. Hell, he was a veteran runaway at this stage in his life. He and any one of his many buddies simply traveled via Santa Fe Railway: it was convenient, cheap, and always had seats available—you just had to be able to run along-side and jump on.

Billy was also a really good escape artist. I remembered one time when the cops were chasing him for some reason. They tried to corral him during a soccer practice at school and thought they had him boxed in on a fenced-in field. But he left those guys standing flat-footed, tunneling under the fence, already three blocks away and gliding over walls like they were hurdles, then dodging between trains parked on the railroad tracks. He was gone!

These family missions to find Dad or Billy were part of Mom's strategy—just keep bringing them back. On that day, back in junior high, our number one mission was to drive around until we found Billy, and number two was to force him to come home. We all knew from experience that these were two entirely different goals with two very different levels of difficulty.

We drove all over town for a couple of hours. My mom knew that I knew the places he might be—that's why I had to come along. We checked everywhere I could think of, but no luck. "C'mon Mom," I said. "It's getting late, I don't think we're gonna find Billy. It'll be all right. You know he'll come home eventually."

We're on a main street, approaching a train crossing, when I suddenly see Billy—he's leaning against a brick wall next to a dilapidated liquor store with his main partner in crime, Steve Larson, no more than thirty or forty yards from us. They're gorging on pies that I later found out they lifted from the store.

Steve is a bad, bad character—white, skinny, long stringy blond hair, unshaven, always wearing the same bell-bottom jeans with a chain hanging from one belt loop to another, and a white t-shirt. Steve is always—and

I mean absolutely *always*—looking for a fight. About five years later, in his early twenties, he was sent to prison on the receiving end of a drug-and-weapons sting operation. Mom read in the paper that he had barricaded himself in his motel room and was surrounded by feds for several hours before surrendering. None of us were surprised. Even in junior high, Steve was a real badass.

They see us in the car at the same time we see them. Mom slams on the brakes—right on the tracks, in the middle of traffic—and yells, "Billy! You get over here, now!"

Billy and Steve drop their pies, look at each other, turn, and run like hell in the opposite direction down the railroad tracks.

But Mom's on a mission. Without missing a beat, my tiny mom kicks off her shoes so they won't get caught in the tracks—she's always thinking ahead—and takes off in pursuit of these two wayward young teens, as if her unyielding will alone could cause them to rethink their impulse to flee. She's running barefoot down the tracks full tilt, paying no heed to the wood chips, the tiny sharp rocks, and the razor-like steel flakes on the rails. Billy just runs further and further away from her. Finally, worn out from screaming and crying, she just crumples to the tracks, exhausted.

I'd been running right along with her, but when she dropped I cut back to the car. We were blocking one of the through lanes across the tracks, and traffic was backed up, the angry drivers honking and yelling. Susie was still just sitting there in the back seat staring at me, tears in her eyes, taking in the whole scene. I felt really bad for her. We were so close back then, and pretty darned aware of what was going on with each other. I knew she was in deep pain, and probably horribly embarrassed.

So when I heard the angry voice from behind me, saying, "Move this piece of crap before I move it for you, you goddamn idiot!" it felt like a punch in the gut.

I turned all my fury and frustration on whoever it was, fist already balled up. "Can't you see we got a family issue goin' on here?" But I'm just eleven, a little kid, so what does this asshole care? He was getting out of his car and coming at me.

"I don't care what you got . . . !"

"Hey! Sit on it, you fat fuck!" I looked as crazy as I could and hope it's convincing enough to make him back off. It works. He got back behind the wheel.

I hopped into the driver's seat of Mom's car and tried to calm my sister down. "It'll be okay, Susie, just relax."

She nodded, okay, probably just hoping I was right. Then I used my secret driving skills—Mom didn't know about these—to pull the car off the road and park it.

I took Susie's hand and we started walking down the tracks. She's my older sister, but I'm the kid who takes care of shit. "C'mon, let's get Mom home."

$$\approx$$

By the time I got to be eleven or twelve it was getting harder and harder to find those innocent, fun kid times on our street. For me and my friends both, life seemed to have darker edges.

One day, when I was walking home from junior high school, I saw a crowd of guys—my brother, his friends and a few of my friends—standing around watching something. I thought maybe it was a fight, and ran over to get in on the action. But as I pushed in closer, I saw my friend, Brian, sitting cross-legged in the dirt, flinging his arms frantically from side to side, like he was trying to use his fingers to see. He had dirt and slobber on his face, and his eyes were rolling back in his head. It was pretty scary.

I looked at Billy. "What's going on?"

"Fuckin' OD-ing," he said. Brian had been snorting Ketamine, a horse tranquilizer and a cheap high. One dollar hit of that would numb your brain out for a couple of hours, like a donkey kicked you in the head. I guessed Brian had gotten hold of more.

Billy, I thought, *I better not catch you like this.*

Brian eventually made it through that seizure and we all helped him get home. But sadly, his brain never acted the same after that day.

And the trestle, too, wasn't so much fun anymore. So many things happened on that damn track. I even had a good neighborhood friend get hit and killed by a passing train. Word was that Gary riding his stingray bike on the tracks—not that uncommon, but he was tripping on LSD at the time. As the train was approaching, Gary thought he could beat it and peddled as hard as he could. The conductor was frantically blowing his horn, but he couldn't slow down tons of iron and steel. Gary was mowed over, pronounced dead on the spot.

My friend Terry's mom came to our junior high school football practice one day. Tears were running down her face, and she had a crumpled tissue in her hand. She told us that our teammate's dad, a police detective, had been shot and killed that afternoon. He was responding to an arrest warrant on a drug suspect. The door opened and he took a bullet point blank to the face.

Sad to say, this kind of thing was part of our everyday life. In my neighborhood, we had lots of drugs, guns, and knife-wielding psychos.

Chapter Four

But somehow, despite people crashing and burning all around me, and coming close to the edge more than a few times myself, I managed to make my own good times. Girls were a mystery to me, but that didn't keep me from being attracted to them. Like most kids, I had crushes on teachers—pretty safe, and always available to look at.

In junior high I had a huge crush on my home ec teacher, a beautiful redhead named Ms. Short. Of course at that age, the only way I knew how to show my undying love was to act like a complete idiot.

I remember one day when she was teaching us how to bake a cake, and I decided it would be hilarious to use my egg for something besides cake batter. I was tossing the egg in the air, smiling at my buddies in the back of the class. Ms. Short was writing out the recipe on the chalkboard, with her face maybe eight inches from the board. I wound up and threw the egg as hard as I could, and the yolk and shells just exploded an inch from her nose. Raw egg all over her. I thought it was great, and so did my friends.

She spins around, really mad, egg and pieces of shell all over her face, eyes blazing, and scans the room. Then—*How did she know?*—she storms straight over to my seat, grabs me, yanks me behind the row of ovens on the side of the room, out of view from most of the class, and just starts leaning in to me, with her finger in my face. I know she was steaming mad, but was there something else weird going on there? I hoped there was. I never found out, but I never forgot it, either.

Despite my antics, or maybe because of them, I was popular in junior high. I was a good athlete, and that always helped with the girls. But my understanding of what it took to make real relationships—even the fleeting first love kind—was nonexistent. I had friends who were girls, but no real girlfriends; just few little make-outs here and there, lots of flirting, the grab-ass kind of stuff that kids do.

My first real kiss was with a friend, Dorothy Alamia, a cheerleader for our junior high football team. We goofed around a fair amount, but I was uncomfortable with the whole girl-as-girlfriend thing. I didn't know how to act or what to say . . . but I did get to first and second base with her and a few others.

The lack of a girlfriend in junior high didn't stop me from having my first sexual encounter, however. Sex was forbidden behavior, so guys had sex with the loose girls rather than have to deal with the stigma or pregnancy issues of a real girlfriend. But in my case, I didn't even plan it; it just happened to me. It may sound like a letter to *Penthouse,* but it ended up kind of traumatic. The whole experience is pretty darn vivid in my mind, even today.

One day, after our junior high baseball game was over, my teammate and good friend Terry Hess and I were hanging out on the outfield fence watching the next game, played by the varsity team. These two girls wandered over to where we were standing and started to talk to us. The one who was really focusing in on me was a couple of years older than me—a girl that all the guys called the "village bicycle" because she'd had a lot of rides.

Before I knew what was happening, we were making out behind the fence, with Terry keeping a lookout. She coaxed me along, one thing led to the next . . . and wow! I was ready, raring to go, *right there.* But then . . . I had absolutely no clue what I was supposed to do. I just stood there, waiting. I thought her thing was like a motor, and it would grab on and do all the work. Clueless!

"What are you waiting for?" she asked me. She was clearly annoyed.

Then she realized I was a virgin, took control, and we did it. Damn, it was a great, but also stressful, I was so awkward and naive. Be careful what you wish for, huh?

By this time, surfing had become another big outlet for all my manic energy. I was desperate to surf, even though we lived at least fifteen miles away from the coast. I'd beg Billy to take me to the beach to surf every chance I got. I didn't care if it was windy, stormy, freezing. . . . Didn't matter, had to surf. Billy loved to surf too, but getting into trouble always won out when he was deciding what to do on a particular day.

One day, though, Billy agreed to help out little bro with transportation out to Oceanside Beach. Bill had just converted his VW Beetle into a Baja Bug—flared fenders, beefy off-road tires, raised four or five inches off the ground, exposed engine in the rear. He was still waiting for the rear shocks and the front grille.

"All right, I'll take you," he told me, "but you know that my fenders rub on the tires if more than two people are in the car."

Rolff Nelson, one of Bill's closest purveyors of trouble in all forms and fashions, was coming with us. So three people in the car was out of the question. Someone needed to ride in the trunk. Rolff and Bill both gave me that look that said, *Yeah you're the little shit that has to do what we say.*

My submission was a foregone conclusion. I just wanted to surf.

A VW bug trunk is in the front and not terribly spacious, to put it mildly, but when you're twelve or thirteen years old, your body is pretty darn flexible and your brain is pretty darn stupid. So I climb in, feet towards the bumper, less than a foot from the pavement, head and shoulders lying flat on top of the gas tank. And Bill and Rolff are laughing and joking about making sure we don't hit anything along the way.

I was laughing right along with them at how stupid the idea was, all the while cussing them out for even mentioning hitting something. And staying put in the trunk. I really wanted to surf. As they pushed the hood down, it pressed hard on my head and shoulders before I finally heard the latch clasp.

"Ow! Watch it!"

"Hey, you better be mellow, dammit!" I could hear their muffled voices in the cab, cackling and joking it up:

"Oh, hey, where's Ronnie?"

"Ah, I don't know, isn't he supposed to be coming with us?"

"I thought so, but where is he?"

You fricken idiots, just drive, it's hard enough just being in here, you boneheads!

"Oh, what's that? I think I hear 'im . . . hold on . . . listen . . . Oh my god, he's in the radio! Ronnie what are you doing in the radio?"

They're laughing hysterically, pounding on the dash, just having a great ol' time. I must say, even being clamped down like a sardine, I was laughing too, but painfully.

Finally, we stopped at a gas station. Oh yeah—I was using my lunch money to pay for their gas. They popped the latch and opened the hood, still cackling as I shielded my eyes from the sudden bright light. As I unfolded myself from the trunk and slowly straightened my cramped arms and legs, the shocked looks on the faces of the other gas buyers made the whole thing pretty funny, even to me. Billy and Rolff were feebly trying to convince me that I should feel lucky to have such a caring brother and friend who had avoided several wrecks with their superhuman driving abilities.

Whatever. I made sure they didn't spill any gas in the trunk, crawled back in, and we were off to surf!

It was a good day for a few hours. But around the middle of the afternoon, as we're all surfing and getting waves, two guys we don't know paddle out near us and start acting like total blockheads. They have shaved skulls and look superfit.

One of the guys keeps going for every wave that I'm going for, and I'm getting more and more irritated. There's an unwritten etiquette to surfing that you understand after you've been doing it for a while: everybody knows who owns the rights to riding what wave, and they don't try to grab it away from you. A lot of times guys who haven't surfed that long don't have any idea about what's acceptable behavior. It's not a crime, but man, there's only the five of us out on this big ocean and plenty of waves! Take your own, or get a better position and take what you want.

Finally, totally fed up, I call the guy out. Our shouting and splashing match turns into an agreement to duel it out on the beach and settle it once and for all. I'm young, but I'm big. So I'm belly-boarding in on my stomach, psyching myself up to twist this guy into a little pretzel until he yells uncle. I get to where the water's about knee-deep, and he's already waiting for me, poised in a wrestling stance. The face-off is fast and furious. My plan to twist him up like a pretzel is not working. Suddenly, it's me on my back underwater, with a death grip on both of his wrists. He's struggling to punch me and I'm struggling to breathe. . . .

And then something very hard and very powerful—Billy's fist—connects with his face. He shoots away from me with such sudden force that his inertia almost pulls me with him. So now it's me, Billy, and Rolff bringing up the rear, against these two angry tough guys, facing off. Then, for no reason, calmer heads prevail, we all back off, and everyone is fine to just call it a day.

Oceanside, where we were surfing that day, is where Camp Pendleton is. After it was all over, we figured out later that these two guys must have been Marines.

"Thanks, bro, damn that guy was quick."

Billy just looks at me and laughs, shaking his head.

~

In 1970, between junior high and high school, Mom shipped fifteen-year-old Billy off to Hawaii. He and his buddies had taken up burglarizing houses, so if he'd stayed in California he'd have gone to juvenile hall for quite some time.

It was weird. They never actually stole anything from these houses; they just broke in when they knew the owners were gone for the weekend or on vacation. Then Bill and his buddies would turn the homes into a kind of clubhouse for partying—eating their food, watching their TV, playing with their hi-fi. They usually left a big mess. When the occupants returned, they invariably called the police, who knew whom to blame.

Billy had twenty-one counts of burglary during his junior high school years. So you can see why he ended up in Hawaii.

Our Hawaiian family went to work and turned Billy into a family rehab project. A lot of Mom's relatives on the mainland and in the islands tried to help her straighten out her oldest son while he was growing up. At one time or another he lived with our uncles Paul, Clarence, and Harold, too. But nothing seem to work very well.

Despite his criminal tendencies, Billy was a great athlete. The uncles tried to make him into a responsible young man by forcing him to play football for McKinley High School. They also tried to straighten him out with responsibility and hard work—he worked for my Uncle Harold's Pacific Island Paper Company, and eventually with our cousin Kamakea in Oahu, back after two tours in Vietnam. But Bill was determined—he just ended up learning how to get in trouble the Hawaiian way instead of becoming responsible. There was plenty of opportunity. One thing he learned to do was ditch school and hang out at the local billiards spots, playing pool for money. Billy became a pretty competent pool shark during that time, sometimes getting into fights to protect his winnings.

By the time he came back home in 1975, two years later, he'd turned Hawaiian. I could hardly understand him when he talked with his new Hawaiian-style pidgin English. I was really happy to have Billy back at home, though. In our neighborhood it was a good thing to have an older brother who could back you up.

While Billy was away, my own athletic career took off. I kept playing baseball, and I'd also started playing football and was kicking ass. Raging hormones were churning up a lot of the energy that had been building over the years, and it felt good to unload it on opposing teams. I guess you'd call full body contact sports a healthy outlet, as opposed to breaking into houses like Billy did. My first team, the Vaqueros, won the league championship and I was the MVP for the season. The next year, we were league champs again, and I was MVP.

Of course my charmed sports career had to end, right?

In 1973, I started Western High School, in Anaheim. Western High was in the CIF, the California Interscholastic Federation, which was a great conference to be in—really good teams. Unfortunately for us, 1973 was also the year they built Cypress High School, which took half our students and some good players. So we got creamed during my years playing football in high school. But never mind,

I loved it anyway. And yeah, I was one of those kids who cried when he lost.

Football was a great release for me. I had a lot of anger, and a bad attitude as a poor Hawaiian kid from the wrong side of the tracks. I got my share of race comments, but I found a way to get back at them. I loved to run full speed at opponents and just crack helmets as hard as I could. I played fullback on offense and linebacker on defense—I always carried the ball or was going after the ball, and always looking to hit someone on the way.

I also got into fights, on and off the field. My coaches tried to downplay it, but they secretly loved the fact that I was so damn aggressive. I'd go psycho and want to kill whoever we were playing against, taking out my misery on the poor guys standing opposite me. It was pretty nuts. I would never give up, even when our team sucked. I would just keep hitting and fighting to the end. The coaches loved it. I could see them smiling and talking it up on the sidelines.

By the ninth grade I was smoking weed, hash, and selling hits of horse tranquilizer— Ketamine. You'd think that having seen my friend Brian OD on the same stuff a couple of years earlier would have cured me, but no. Selling it was really stupid, although I honestly thought it was no big deal. I just wanted to unload enough to buy this Infinity surfboard I had my eyes on, and that would be it. My big plan. It seemed logical at the time.

But the principal, Mr. Muncie, got wind of my business, and called me in to his office. I was such a hot athlete that I honestly didn't think the school would challenge me on anything, so I didn't even bother removing the dozen hits in little bindles in my pocket. I sat down at Muncie's desk and he asked me to empty my pockets.

I couldn't believe it. Now I was really in deep trouble. I was so pissed. Someone betrayed me! Looking back, it probably didn't take anyone to turn me in. I was so blatant about it, I wonder if I actually wanted to get caught.

I put the bindles on his desk and we didn't talk much. A police officer showed up, out of nowhere, and the next thing I knew I was cuffed and walking through campus for everyone to see. I went straight to juvenile hall for a week. Usually, they release you on OR, your "own recognizance," within three days, but they considered what I had a very dangerous drug.

Mom and Dad came to visit. Mom was distraught. She asked, "Why? How could you possibly do this? Who put you up to it? Was it Billy again?"

"No," I told them. "It wasn't Billy. It was no one else, it was just me."

They were furious, and confused. I was supposed to be the good son, or at least the better son. Why would I do such a crazy thing? When I told them the truth—I wanted a new surfboard—I don't think they ever really believed it. It did sound kind of stupid.

But when I got out of juvenile hall, Dad bought me the very board I had been saving up for.

Talk about your mixed messages.

Usually high school is pretty stratified—you are known by who you hang out with. But I seemed to cross all the cliques. I was friends with the jocks, the surfers, the loadies, and even few of the Vatos, a Mexican gang at our school. Team sports let you cross lines, since some guys were drawn to a sport even though they had an affiliation with a gang or a particular group.

I was still going full speed ahead when it came to acting out my anger. Even though I had some friends who were Vatos, I had other friends who weren't—and we got into some big standoffs with them. A buddy of mine took a knife in the forearm protecting himself during one gang brawl. Hordes of cops would show up when we had the big standoffs at lunch, or after school. We were lucky—that was in the days before every kid had a gun.

And my adventures with drugs didn't stop either. I got stoned at lunch almost every day—which made school less educational but more enjoyable—right up to the end. One of my best friends and I took a hit of acid for our last high school football game. Tripping during warm-ups, Tommy and I were pushing it to the edge, as usual. What did we have to lose? Nothing. Go for it, bro! We didn't care. We did what we did, and a lot of it.

I was popular in high school, was voted homecoming king and all that, but I was still sort of shy and didn't try too hard when it came to girls. I didn't like all the work involved, at least that's what I would have said then. It came off as aloof. Now, I think I was just too insecure. I couldn't figure out why they would like me, or what they could possibly see in me, so I rarely noticed when they sent me signals. Girls would think that if you're hanging together, then you're an exclusive item, but I didn't. I was a shark; always moving.

One of my first real girlfriends in high school was Leslie Shaw, "Shawbones." She was a good skateboarder and surfer—all my friends' favorite girl! She was like one of the guys. She went everywhere with us, partying. I think I was her first, and she was pretty head over heels, a lot more serious about it than I was then.

My next real girlfriend, though, was something else. A girl from the other side of the tracks, the right side. Her name was Nicole Brown—yes, *that* Nicole Brown. She was just a high school girl, fifteen years old. But she was a knockout!

Nicole and I met in the winter or early spring of 1974. My buddies and I had been fooling around at Hillcrest, a big park in Fullerton with huge hills and paved roads that were ideal for our Big Wheel races. We'd race four or five guys at a time on these three-wheeled plastic kids toys, shooting down steep hills and around sharp corners, scaring motorists who were surprised to see big guys on Big Wheels flying by them, even right at them. These sessions always ended in the same way: the cops showed up and told us to go home.

On this day, we got chased out early. But it was a nice, warm sunny afternoon, and we all decided to go to a party in Anaheim, at a friend's house.

I was hanging around partying, having a good time, when my friend Dana nodded in the direction of this beautiful blonde girl across the room. "Dude, she wants to hook up."

I look at her, and sure enough she's staring at me. It still wasn't registering. I look back at Dana, pointing my finger at my own chest.

"Me?"

"Yeah!" He shakes his head and laughs. "Dude, she's all over you dude!"

I could not believe it—this girl was just perfect. I thought, *Wow, insane!* She was just so striking, really beautiful. I was hooked the moment we locked eyes across the room.

Her personality was pretty awesome too. She was friendly and fun, but not overly enthusiastic about anything. And she didn't go out of her way to meet people.

Pretty quickly, Nicole and I started going out—puppy love. Nothing was said, but we always assumed we would be together when we would see each other at a party or concert or whatever. I'm not sure if we ever talked about being exclusive, but we were drawn to each other, spending lots of time together just being together and hanging out.

Nicole had two younger sisters, Mini and Tonya, and an older sister, Denise—another knockout, and a real model. In fact, Denise was on the cover of *Cosmopolitan* magazine right about the time I met Nicole. All the guys I knew wanted to be associated with Nicole and Denise. Who wouldn't? And of course, there was talk. Everyone seemed to want to volunteer how far they had gotten with Nicole or Denise, or even with their mom, who was also beautiful. I thought it was all pretty bizarre. I let the rumors go in one ear and out the other. Nicole and I had a genuine connection, even if I didn't know exactly how to handle it.

Nicole loved to come to my baseball games. I remember the last game of the season, when Nicole and pretty much my whole family were in the stands watching and I took one in the family jewels. I was a catcher and hated wearing cups—too confining, especially when I was batting.

Anyhow, my buddy Terry was pitching and he had a serious fast ball. Long story short: tipped bat, just below my glove, my left nut is dead to this day. I was laid out on the field for ten minutes. My mom, Auntie Ruth, my friends, Nicole—all of them had to go to the hospital with me after the game. I got a huge amount of personal sympathy from Nicole after that incident, which was very nice.

As we spent more and more time together, Nicole wanted me to meet her family and their friends. I went to a couple of her parent's parties—they had a big house in Garden Grove with a tennis court, swimming pool, huge yard, the whole package. I was very uncomfortable being with all these affluent people, young and old. I had no idea how to mix with wealthy people—it was a whole different world. But I felt like it was important to Nicole, so I tried.

I still don't know how her family felt about me. They probably did, or didn't really care one way or the other, but the way my mind worked at the time, I thought they couldn't possibly like me. I was just too different, too Hawaiian from the wrong side of the tracks and all. The girls' father, Mr. Brown, was Midwestern, a serious man of few words. He never had any bad words for me, but he never said anything encouraging either, especially as it related to Nicole.

I was super shy around them. I didn't look people directly in the eyes when I talked to them, which I know now comes from deep insecurity. Once when I had dinner at her house with her family, I was nervous and accidentally spilled my milk. I was so embarrassed that I remember it to this day, but they didn't make much out of it.

Meanwhile things between Nicole and me were going really well. But at that crucial moment my mom's family invited me (or maybe it was Mom's plan) to stay with them on Oahu and surf my brains out all summer. Better, I could take my friends.

I loved being with Nicole, but I never accepted that she wanted to be with me. If I'd had even a reasonable idea of how to express myself, we would have had a much longer, more meaningful relationship. Instead, I took off for the islands with three of my surfing buddies, Steve Whitaker, Jesse Crowthers, and Steve Houston.

Chapter Five

My uncles picked up the two Steves, Jesse, and me at the airport, but primarily this was a kids surfing trip. I always knew I could count on my Hawaiian cousins for help if I needed it, but we wanted to be on our own. So all four of us decided to stay at this little cottage in the jungle on Oahu's northeast shore. It was owned by Mrs. Naii, a super-old Chinese Hawaiian lady, the mother of my mom's best friend from Hawaii. She was great.

Jesse and Steve Whitaker got off to a rough start, though—and on our first night at Mrs. Naii's place. It was so secluded, we thought, no worries. So when we went to get something to eat, Steve and Jesse left two of their boards sitting out on the porch. Jesse had a brand new Beatty, red with light red flames on the deck, and Whitaker's was used, but a decent board. Bad move for both of them. Both boards were gone when we got back, and they never saw them again.

Bummer!

Still, even Steve and Jesse didn't let it bother them for too long. They borrowed some old boards from my cousins. This trip was just too perfect. Back home, the only way to get to the beach was to get a ride with someone older or hitchhike, which was pretty common—and pretty safe—back then. I'd even take the bus when I was desperate. In Hawaii, we paid a dime each day to take the bus to surf the best spots—Ala Moana Bowls, Three's, Kaisers, In Betweens, Magic Islands. . . . We were in heaven.

On those rare days that we didn't surf, we'd still end up at the beach, trying our hand at spearfishing. Which wasn't easy. We were total novices, and in Hawaii you typically don't use a spear gun. You typically use a Hawaiian sling, which is a long shaft with a three-prong spear on one end and surgical tubing on the other. It was absolutely comical trying to catch eels or ink-spewing octopus for the first time. But we gave it our all, and we proudly came back to Miss Naii with an occasional octopus or a bite-size fish, and she would dutifully prepare it for us or teach us how to prepare it for grilling on our Hibachi cooker.

We all had really long hair in those days, which sometimes drew unwanted attention. But I looked Hawaiian, so I never got hassled. My three friends were a different story, though—they were obviously *haoles,* white boys from the mainland. Steve Houston in particular had superlong blond hair. That went over great in Southern California, but in Hawaii those guys got some of the biggest stink eye ever by the big local guys.

For some reason, it hadn't occurred to me that being Hawaiian with mainland *haole* friends was going to be complicated, but it was. Hawaiians are basically dependent on the tourist industry—the despised *haoles*—because without it unemployment would be rampant. It's viewed as a necessary evil, taking the bad along with the good, but it's a struggle. A good percentage of the population is happy to have gainful employment, but underneath is a constant resentment that can't be totally submerged.

On my previous trips to Hawaii, I'd watched my bigger cousins down a few beers at a family gathering, getting angrier by the minute. They'd say to me, "'Ey Ronny boy, you like go buss some *haole* heads, bra?"

What do you do when you're from both sides of the aisle—part Hawaiian, part German and Scottish, as cornbread hillbilly as they come? It's tough to stay neutral, trying to be friends with both sides. Going back and forth from California to Hawaii, with two separate roles to play, led to a pretty mixed-up identity and some weird experiences.

One day on that summer trip, we missed the last bus coming back from a surfing town on the South Shore and got stranded in the middle of nowhere. And, of course, it was raining. We're standing there, getting wetter by the minute, trying to figure out how we're going to get home.

Then we see these big Hawaiian Samoans—and I mean really big—hanging out down the street from the bus stop where we got dropped off. Jesse and the two Steves made a point of ignoring them. But the Samoans take a long look at Steve Houston's hair and one of them yells, "Eh blonde, I like fuck you, bra!"

The Samoans started walking our way. We were all a bit freaked, but Steve was just wiggin' out. I had no idea what we would do, but I could already feel my hands balling up into fists.

And then a miracle happened.

This old white Rambler pulls up next to us, and a cool Hawaiian dude and his girlfriend motion us to jump in. He was smoking a big fat joint to boot. We didn't waste a second making up our minds. We mashed ourselves into the back seat of the Rambler, looking over our shoulders at the Samoans, who were still slowly walking our way.

"Eh, you guys stuck or what, brah?" Our new Hawaiian driver looks at us through his rear view mirror, smoke curling up from his joint as he pulls away from the bus stop.

We shift around, looking back at the Samoans and relishing our good fortune as they yell at us and flip us off, their good times ruined.

"Oh, brah," I say to our savior, "thanks so much for picking us up. Those dudes were about to impregnate Steve here, man. Damn . . . so lucky!"

"Eh, no worries, brah." Our driver grins. "They cannot run, brah, they neva catch!"

He hands his joint back to us, without looking. Then, one hand on the wheel, he speeds down the dark, curvy, rain-soaked road, whipping around the turns.

He's jabbering away about the locals and what to expect and why and you got to be careful just don't do stupid stuff like being loud and annoying—my friends pretty much had that covered, I thought. The stupidest thing you could do was "drop in" on the local guys—catch a wave from the shoulder that was already taken by another surfer in the deep part. Big no-no. I took it all to heart.

Finally, our roller coaster ride home comes to an end. Thoroughly stoned now, and anxious to get inside out of the rain, we yell our thanks again and jump out. We run through the jungle to our little hovel among the trees, glad to have gotten home with all of our body parts intact.

Ala Moana Bowls, with its perfect waves, was the most popular surf spot on the South Shore during the summer months. It was always packed with the serious local surfers—Ben Aipa, Buttons Kaluhiokalani, Larry Bertlemann, and so many others. These guys were heavyweights. Bertlemann is a legend. Kaluhiokalani is credited with inventing modern surfing. And Aipa, a monster competitor who didn't even start surfing until he was twenty-five, shaped boards and innovated the short board that changed everything.

The correct behavior would be to drop to your knees in front of these guys, saying, *I'm not worthy! Everybody* knew that you don't just drop in take a wave from one of the locals, *especially* not one of these guys. But noooooo. . . . It wasn't one of us three that made that giant error, but it was our very good buddy Dan.

Dan was older than us, but we knew him from the old neighborhood, back in Buena Park. He had moved to Oahu just a couple of months before we got there to surf to his heart's content. Dan was a good surfer, and he was a really cool guy—he even let us leave our boards at his house, which was about ten blocks from our favorite surf spot at Ala Moana. So we would catch the bus from country to town every morning and then catch the last bus back in the evening. But I guess his coolness only went so far.

On this one perfect, sunny day, I watched Dan drop in on the last local surfer you ever wanted to drop in on back then, Ben Aipa. Dan told me later that he just couldn't stop himself. It was the best wave he'd ever seen, big and perfect. He just wasn't going to let it go.

I watched Dan and Aipa paddle back out after they took the wave. Dan got back out first, then Aipa. Aipa's not real tall, but he's got more than ten years on us teenagers and he's thick as a brick—like a brown Michelin Man with surf trunks on. I could see Dan scrambling immediately. "Dude, I swear, I didn't see you I didn't know you were there!" He was talking as fast as he could. Aipa didn't say a word, which was even more terrifying.

The legend just paddled up to Dan, grabbed him by the neck like a chicken, popped him one time hard in the face, then put him back on his board, said a few words, and paddled out again.

Just like that. BOOM! Over, done.

Dan just sat there, holding his eye.

"What'd Aipa say to you, dude?" I asked him when he got back to shore with us.

Dan just shook his head, holding his eye: "I'm not allowed to surf Ala Moana Bowls for the rest of the summer."

Ahh, Ala Moana.

By the time I got back from my summer adventure, things between me and Nicole had cooled off a little bit but we were still together. Around this time her family moved from Garden Grove to Monarch Beach in South Laguna, and I began to meet and hang out with some of her new, wealthy friends.

In Southern California, where you are what you drive, it seemed to me that every one of her friends' parents drove a Mercedes or a Porsche or an Audi or a Cadillac. My world was Ford Galaxies, AMC Ramblers, and Chevy Impalas. I was completely out of my element, but I kept paddling.

At first, I thought her family and her affluent friends must have a great life, much better than what I was used to. It certainly looked good to me. Plus, people weren't yelling at each other (at least where I could hear them), or throwing things at each other, or getting hauled off by the cops. Nicole's family and friends seemed more in control of their destinies.

Slowly, though, the more I got to know these kids, I began to see the cracks. A whole host of other insecurities plagued these well-off folks. These weren't the concerns I knew about: making your mortgage payment on time, not being able to afford Christmas gifts one year, or trying to hide the fact that your dad is a raging alcoholic nutcase. It was more hidden and even more warped, I thought, because these people had everything—plenty of food, access to a comfortable lifestyle, big houses, expensive cars, lavish parties. But, as time went on, I began to see this exciting new world I had become a part of as steeped with discontent and mental anguish.

One case like this was a girl I met at one of Nicole's parties named Kris Kumer. When I first met Kris, she was in a big fight with her parents. She had actually left her parents' home and was living with her friend Maryanne. I thought, *How weird.* This girl had everything. How could she and her parents actually have a problem so severe that it drove them apart? But her story was pretty common.

I thought about my mom, chasing her husband and kids all through town every other day just to try to keep us all in the same house. And my parents, dysfunctional as they were, were still together. Yet it seemed like all the kids that I met through Nicole had parents who were divorced, or whose kids didn't like them. The parents *and* kids were in and out of therapy constantly. The parents were taking tons of antidepressants, and the kids would steal the pills and give them out to their friends.

I couldn't understand these people. Didn't everyone have grievances they needed to work out with each other?

Finally, Nicole and I parted ways. It was never the same after I got back from Hawaii. With my lack of self-confidence, I figured she was more interested in her new friends and, probably, new boyfriends. Looking back, I can see that she actually did give me some reason to put effort into being with her, but I was afraid of what might happen if I let myself really fall head over heels for her. Wary and untrustworthy from being let down so much in life, my aloof attitude probably just wore her out. I loved being with Nicole, but never accepted that she wanted to be with me. If I'd had even a reasonable idea of how to express myself, we would have had a much longer, more meaningful relationship.

I regret that quite a bit. If nothing else, I wish I had been raised with enough confidence to seize great things when they presented themselves to me . . . So many opportunities, with no clue how to take advantage of them. It was sad about Nicole and me.

A couple of years after that, when she was eighteen, Nicole met O.J. Simpson. Over the years, after she was married to O.J., I would run into Nicole at the beach or in the neighborhood. She was afraid to do more than just say hi or bye. O.J. was always lurking around, and he would just grill her if he thought something was up with some other guy. I thought at the time it was kind of freaky.

I went to her funeral, right after the murder. For my money, O.J. was guilty as guilty gets. He was there and said nothing, just a blank stare. At the burial site, nothing. No emotion, no expression. And then he went on that famous highway chase in his White Ford Bronco. . . . For a while I beat myself up thinking that if I hadn't been so shy, maybe Nicole and I would have been able to make a serious go of it and she would have never ended up with O.J.

Sad thoughts.

Chapter Six

In 1976, out of the blue, my Dad announced that we were buying a house in Costa Mesa, just a couple of miles from the Pacific Ocean. I was elated. Closer to the beach!

At this point, Dad had actually been sober for a couple of years. Sobriety had apparently allowed him to get his act together, get some jobs done, and make some money. Much to my amazement, he sold our house in Buena Park for a small fortune.

Good for my dad, I thought. Look what you can accomplish with sobriety. I wish he'd started sooner!

Dad had finally got sober on about his third try through rehab. My big sister Susie got the ball rolling—she made it clear to Mom that she couldn't take his drunken bullshit anymore. When Susie finally got mad, you had to pay attention.

She rallied us boys to go with her to Mom as a united force. Susie told her that all of us kids were ready to move to Hawaii to live with relatives if Dad's shenanigans didn't stop. Susie was serious. She even lined up agreements from our relatives in Hawaii about who would live with who.

Gathered and ready, we approached my mom. Susie did all the talking. Mom could be pretty tough on Susie, so I know it took a lot of guts for Susie to stand up to her.

Mom got the message loud and clear: you choose your kids or you choose your husband. This time, it worked. She chose us, and Dad went to rehab.

The new house had enough room for Dad to park all his paving equipment. But more important for him, it also had room for a horse corral at the bottom of the bluff, about fifty feet down, at the base of the low-lying area that eventually empties out at River Jetties. River Jetties divides two of the largest beach towns in Orange County, Newport and Huntington. There were trails throughout this area that flanked a canal, most of it winding through brush, trees, and massive clumps of bamboo.

My dad had always had an interest in horses from growing up on a farm in the hills of North Carolina, where they were commonplace. It was a dream of my Dad's to have a big ranch with horses everywhere. This was a start.

Billy was a horse guy too, like Dad, although it didn't bring them any closer together. And even though Dad was sober, he was even more of a dick to Bill now. He just scowled at Bill every chance he got. Not to say that Bill didn't instigate stuff. They were in it together by this time.

Not too long after the move, Dad did a paving job for an attorney who paid part of his bill in the form of a race horse called Sissy—she didn't have a track name because after a couple of trail races at Los Alamitos, it was clear that she couldn't be trusted.

Naturally, Billy loved this horse on sight.

"Dude," he told me, "guaranteed this mare is easily the most beautiful quarter horse I've ever seen. Bro! The thing stands seventeen hands, minimum. She's a deep chestnut, with the longest blonde mane you've ever seen. On top of that, the fucker has got a look in her eye like, *Maaaan, you better be ready for some shit if you think you're jumping on my back.* I shit you not, bro.

"*Shiiiit* dude, can't wait to ride this bitch!"

Billy was feeling that adrenaline rush just thinking about riding this mare.

A few days later, Billy was sitting on the fence rail, enjoying the sunny day with Moki, our goofy giant of a dog, a German shepherd–Rottweiler cross, at his feet. Billy and Moki were watching Dad with the trainer, who was attempting to work his magic with the stubborn animal. This guy was actually the eighth trainer to try his hand with this beautiful but ornery mare. Dad wasn't a very forgiving personality, and if things didn't go his way, he could be every bit as ornery as the beast he was attempting to tame. But I guess this trainer was okay, because he lasted a while.

Well, the trainer finally finished. Dad had a short, frank discussion with him and came over to Billy. Dad stared hard at him, one eyebrow raised. That look meant, *You better damn well listen to every word that comes out of my mouth, or else!*

What he said was, "Billy, you are not to take this horse out of this corral for any reason, do you understand me? This is the eighth trainer I've had to hire and I don't want you messing that up. You hear?"

"Yeah, I hear ya."

"Good," said Dad, narrowing his eyes and looking hard to make sure Billy got the point.

Finally, he figured Billy really did get the point, and left, saying he had to bid on some jobs.

As Dad walked back up the trail, Billy looked down at Moki and said, "Today we ride."

Today. We. Ride.

That was Billy all the way.

As soon as the trainer left and Dad was out of sight, Billy grabbed the saddle and bridle and threw them on the mare. Then he hopped on her back and ran Sissy through her paces—figure eights, reverse, and a few other maneuvers. It looked pretty good. "Damn, she's great," Billy said.

He looked over at Moki again and said, "Yeah, today we ride."

Even Moki must have known this was not a great idea.

But Billy can't wait. He jumps on Sissy's back, unlatches the gate, and she jumps into a gallop. *Holy shit!* Billy pulls her up and stops to adjust the stirrups. Sissy takes the opportunity to graze on some grass.

Billy pulls on the reins. "Let's go!" But Sissy just turns her head and shoots a glance at Bill as if to say, *WHAT?* And goes right back down and grabs another huge mouthful of lush green grass.

Billy yanks at the reins again—she has to know who's in charge here. But the massive horse rears straight back and up, hard and fast. Right as he's about to fly off he grabs at the long blond mane and manages to get a good enough hold to stay on her back. At that, she suddenly lunges forward and bolts back toward home base, like the racehorse she could have been.

Now they're rushing along the narrow trail, in and out of bamboo, brush, and trees. According to what Billy told me later, Sissy is clearly working hard to scrape him off her back, but he's hanging onto her mane and squeezing his legs tighter. Staying on her back is taking every bit of strength he's got.

In no time at all they circle around and are almost back where they started, going about a thousand miles an hour. And Sissy's not slowing down. *Damn, she's keeping this up until she flings my ass like a rag doll,* he was thinking. But all he could do was hang on.

As they come through the last clump of bamboo, Billy sees certain either salvation or certain death—a six-foot-high pile of dirt, rock, and broken-up concrete and asphalt across from the corral gate on the right side of the trail. *That's it.*

He reaches as high up on the mane as possible with one hand, grabs more mane with the other hand, and cranks down to his right side as hard as he can. Now Sissy has no choice but to follow her head down—throwing Billy head over heels. . .

Free at last, Sissy comes to a screeching halt.

Billy—being Billy—lands on his feet on the rubble heap with not a single scratch or bruise. "Whoa, that was nuts!"

My big brother has many faults, but being boring is not one of them.

Beyond all reason, Dad kept Sissy. Later, he bred her, and she had a foal that he named I'm a Cute Gal. After he sold her, Sissy's filly actually did race at Los Alamitos race track.

∾

The constant craziness in our house only hit me later, when I was in college, far enough away that it was disturbing rather than normal. I'd stand under the shower, water running over my head and face after a long day of surfing and studying or class and basketball. *Ahhh . . .*

Then suddenly, I'd hear screaming and yelling.

I'd pull my head out of the pounding water and listen more intently. Nothing.

Back under the water, more yelling and screaming.

Fuck! What the ... ?

It dawned on me over time that I was so used to hearing screaming and fighting while I was in the shower I imagined I was hearing it when it wasn't there.

My showers back in Buena Park must have been a refuge for me. Escape under the water when everything was cracking up around you. I think surfing was an extension of my solitude in the shower. In water, away from all the crap, the silence was beautiful. I could surf for hours and hours, even if it was freezing cold!

Some of my parents' fights were pretty nasty. Mom defending herself with some sharp object, us kids pleading for them to stop. . . . Nasty. And pretty embarrassing when the cops came out to tell them to keep it down, which happened all the time.

As early as five or six years old, I used to fall asleep with a knife pressed to my stomach, hoping I would one night have the courage to do it, to end their fighting and screaming once and for all.

I tried to burn out my frustration on football, but by high school my anger was boiling over. Around then I got arrested for the second time in my life, for assault on a police officer. And on Halloween night, no less.

I was dressed up like a sorcerer, tripping on acid, and having a fine time at a party in Huntington Beach. This party, however, turned into a riot, complete with German shepherd police dogs and helicopters.

When the police started marching forward, everyone let their beer bottles fly, including me. We started running away as fast as we could at that point, but these two biker-looking guys started trailing us. They made a grab at me, so I squared up and cracked one of them. They wrestled me to the ground and beat the living bejesus out of me.

Turns out these guys were undercover cops.

Then they smashed my bloody face against the paddy wagon, leaving a big blood smear on the white paint of the wagon as my face went slowly down.

When we got back to the station and they found out I was only seventeen, the cops freaked. They had just beaten a minor to pulp. I counted eight lumps and cuts on my head and face the next morning, and passed out cold later in the day.

Mom and Billy came to the police station to get me out of jail. Billy—all too familiar with police—almost jumped through the protective glass window when he saw me.

The cops were pretty sheepish about making such a mess out of my face, and let him get away with saying a lot of derogatory stuff that normally wouldn't fly.

Bill was pretty protective of little bro back then!

∽

Towards the end of my high school career, Billy started taking me to bars with his friends. They were a crazy group.

Truly "prime-time, disco shine." *Everybody* was "kung fu fightin'" all the time.

One night, we're walking out of this joint, the Purple Lounge or something like that, and we see two groups facing each other, exchanging insults. One good-sized guy is jabbing his finger into the chest of a friend of my brother's, little Jimmy Johnson, who's no slouch for a little dude.

We walk up and decide to act like police for a change. I take the lead and come up next to little Jimmy. I point at his assailant with my own finger, telling him to pick on someone his own size or mellow out. We're going back and forth, checking the scene out of the corner of my eye to see what our odds are, when BAM!

Out of nowhere one of their guys cold cocks me hard enough to make my head swing back. By the time my head returns to its normal position, I'm sober, alert, and ready to hunt. The dude is jumping up and down in front of me with his dukes up like Muhammed Ali. I decide to use one of Bill's surprise warfare techniques to disarm my opponent before I strike.

"What's up with you crackin' me like that when I'm tryin' to help everyone! Just stay cool."

I'm working hard to convince the guy that I don't want to fight, I'm just here trying to break it up. Finally, the knucklehead drops his dukes—and I let him have a really big one right in the chops.

Now all hell breaks loose, with both sides going after each other. Unfortunately, I've managed to let someone get me in a headlock. But Billy throttles the guy, who loses his grip and allows me to return some trauma. Billy's always got my back.

At the same time, though, I can see that some big beast of a dude is lurching towards big brother. Billy feints a couple of steps, as if running away. As the guy lunges forward face first, Bill pivots on his right foot and delivers a bomb that drops the guy straight to the ground, a technique he told me later Uncle Clarence had taught him in Hawaii. In any case, the beast falls like a redwood tree, cracking his head on a parking stop for good measure. Flat on his face in a pool of blood.

Party's over. Cops are arriving from all sides, and everybody scrambles.

Billy kept an eye out for little bro if he was anywhere in the vicinity—and even when he wasn't. He and his absolutely insane friends held such a reputation that most people preferred to steer clear of them.

I'd sympathize with Bill and his friends when they'd get harassed over anything that happened, complaining that they were unfairly singled out whether they were responsible or not.

"It's not right! It's a violation of our constitutional rights," they'd always complain.

"Yeah, that's right, you can't just question me for no reason without any evidence or proof. You know the law says 'innocent until proven guilty,' don't it? Hahaaaaa! Gotcha—now leave me alone before I call your boss and have your badge confiscated."

I'd actually hear Bill talk to cops like that while one of his friends was sneezing out the word "piggy" or "porky" in the background. Sometimes they'd get roughed up for it, and sometimes not.

Back then, it didn't dawn on me just how their careless, seemingly suicidal attitude percolated through the minds of the general population. Eventually, I realized that the cops knew what doors to knock on when something crazy happened. Ours was definitely one of them.

Tutu's family before she was born. Left to right: Her mom Fannie and father, William Chee Sung Han, and in front brothers Billy, Johnny, and Jimmy.

Dad's family in 1938, two years before his mother passed away. Left to right: Dad's sister Rose, Dad, sister Gene, Grandpa and Grandma McElroy.

Dad, back in the hills of North Carolina early growing years—
later 1930's.

Grandpa William Ryan McElroy on his boat, around 1940, just
after his wife, my grandmother, passed away from cancer. My
Dad was eleven.

Dad in the Navy, 1952, while on tour throughout the Mediterranean.

Uncle Clarence while playing football for Iolani all boys high school in Honolulu in 1952. He went on to play for Compton College and Idaho State.

Another Hula from
Mom. California,
late1950s.

Brothers, 1962, on the porch
Buena Park. Big brother Bill
and Little brother Ronnie.

Early McElroy Family: Dad, Susan, Bill, Ron, and Tutu.

North Shore, Oahu-1976

Uncle Jimmy, Aunty Kalama, and kids Jane and Patrick in Molokai in 1977. That's me on the right, just out of high school.

My sister Susan, nineteen years old in 1978, just before leaving for the cult.

Surfing in Fiji 1994. Perfect cloud-break days with friends.

Liz
Playa Loma Bonita, 2008.

Brett, Cameron, and me with brand new just born baby Lock.
Newport Beach 2004.

Daughter Lockley.

Chapter Seven

For a while there, I was keeping up with Billy when it came to stupid, reckless behavior. One time in particular still gives me the shivers to think about.

Just after high school, Susie met this cool guy, Mike, who was just back from Vietnam, kind of a lean, Brad Pitt–good looking dude. He was the first guy that Susie had gone out with that stuck around for a while. Mike and I would hang out a bit when he was over, and one day we got to talking about his time in Vietnam. About the mayhem, but also about the drugs. Specifically, the heroin.

He said that you just gradually accept heroin as part of life in Vietnam because since things are so screwed up over there. Then after you try it, and get past the idea that doing heroin is crossing a line, it actually helps you understand things that you didn't before.

He managed to convince me that heroin was a cool drug—and he just happened to be carrying.

Well, okay.

We took off in the '65 VW bug that I had by that time, with me driving. It was calm, sunny afternoon as we pulled into this park. People were hitting balls back and forth on a tennis court, a couple was throwing a Frisbee back and forth . . . normal weekend activity. Plus heroin.

Mike pulls out his rig. He ties my arm off with a surgical tube, and cooks up the heroin in a little spoon. Then he draws it into his syringe and tells me to relax.

BAM! *Whoa . . . slow motion. . . .* It seems like I leaned back but didn't move. . . . I'm trying to focus as Mike preps himself for a hit, . . . Mike just falls over forward onto the dashboard, collapsed.

Whoa! I'm still leaning back but not moving.
Fuck.

I sat there for I don't know how long.

Then I decided that I needed to move. It took me forever to open the door, which was light as a tin can. Mike was still slumped over, needle still in his arm.

I stepped out of the car . . . *Whoa, my legs are soooo looong . . . Wow, people playing in park* . . . I take a few steps . . . sit down. . . .

I'm not sure how long I sat there, but finally I decided it was time to get up and do something about Susie's boyfriend.

I struggled back behind the wheel and started the car, ready to go. I knew I was close to the apartment Billy was living in then. I don't know how I did it, but I managed to drive and actually park in my brother's complex.

Mike is still slumped over.

I'm thinking, *Wow, is he breathing? Is he dead? Fuck. What'll I do?*
Billy will know what to do.

I barely make it to his front door. Thank God Billy lived on the ground floor. As soon as I knock on his door, though, I keel over into the ivy next to the porch and start a violent, unending puke.

Billy opens the door, already yelling at me. "Fuck! I told you not to do that shit, you fucking idiot!" He knew exactly what was going on, I didn't need to say anything.

Between pukes, I managed to blurt out, "I think Michael's dead, he's in the car."

"Get inside," Billy said, shoving me into the apartment. He went to look at Mike, who was still breathing. Billy hauled him into the house behind me and we both spent a while on our backs getting our heads on straight. It took a few hours before I was ready to take Mike back to my big sister.

⁓

Here's the Susie I grew up with: One day she called home, crying. She'd rear-ended a car and hit her head on the steering wheel. But that was not what she was crying about. She was upset because our dog Coco, a medium-sized German shepherd–Husky mix was with her and she thought she'd injured the dog.

I jumped in my car and sped to her accident, a few blocks away. Coco was fine and Susie had a bloody lip, but nothing serious. *Kind and sweet, kind and sweet,* that's all I can think of when I think of my sister.

Susie had even more trouble with male-female relationships than I did. She was beautiful, inside and out, with long hair all the way down her back, and guys noticed. As she got older and was dating more, she seemed to fall hard when she first started dating—junior high school captain of the football team, high school CIF all-state quarterback—but it didn't last. I think it really bummed her out. She didn't know how to act or express herself when it came to a relationship. How could she? She had no example to follow.

Then something happened to Susie that sent her off the deep end. It was only recently that I learned the whole sad, awful story. Sometimes, I wonder: if Mom hadn't gotten Dad into rehab that third time, and we kids did pack up and move to Hawaii, would the story have taken a brighter turn? Although by that time, Susie was so sensitive, and damaged, that it could have ended up even worse than it did.

Just after high school, Susie had gotten pregnant with Mike's baby. At first, she hid the pregnancy from Mom. I think she wanted to keep the baby, but Mike wasn't too happy about it. So, late in the pregnancy, she just gave in to the pressure. Like so many girls back then—abortion was still illegal—she ended up going to some back alley quack to abort it. The abortion was so late that they had to infuse some sort of solution, essentially killing the fetus.

When Susie delivered the aborted fetus it looked just like a little baby, but like had been burned alive. The "medical" person made her take a good look at it, to "teach her a lesson." She freaked out and never really got over it, in my opinion.

After that, Susie started attending these "Bible studies" at the Tony and Susan Alamo Christian Foundation in Hollywood. Alamo was this strange guy who was also known at the time for selling sequined "Tony Alamo" jackets. Basically, he was a con man and a nutcase. But for Susie, he was the head of her new family.

A couple of times, I caught glimpses of her and her friends speaking in tongues. It freaked me out. After that, I had recurring dreams of being possessed by the devil. I was just a kid myself. I couldn't rescue her. To preserve my own sanity, I just kept doing my thing and let her do her thing.

In 1976, shortly after her nineteenth birthday, she told us that she couldn't speak to us any longer because we were "people of the world." Mom was devastated.

Soon after, Mike left her and she joined a cult—a polygamous "religious" commune, the Tony and Susan Alamo Christian Ministries Foundation. Susie married a fellow cult member, and had two sons.

After that, this foundation had a series of calamitous setbacks. Susan Alamo died of cancer in 1982, and in 2009, Tony was convicted of transporting minors for illegal sexual purposes, rape, and sexual assault, and sentenced to 175 years in prison. But throughout the long and terrible history of this cult, Susie remained a true believer. She left once, briefly, and then went back. More than thirty-five years later now, Susie's still there.

Susie always was loyal. Now she's loyal to her adopted family to a fault, regardless of her bonds of marriage or children. At the beginning, when she first went in, we thought about kidnapping her and hiring deprogrammers. But we never did.

We were all so screwed up ourselves, how did we know if Susie was worse off than us?

~

High school was rapidly becoming almost nonexistent for me. I got to the point where I was so bored with it I just didn't care about working hard or even taking the sports as seriously as I did before.

One of my best friends, Tommy, and I didn't think anything of taking a hit of acid for our last game of high school football. Tripping during warm-ups, we were pushing it to the edge, as usual during those days. What did we have to lose? Nothing. Go for it, bro!

LSD and football, as it turned out, did not mix well. During warm-ups it was kind of fun. Tommy and I were doing jumping jacks next to each other, glancing from side to side, tripping on all the waving arms and lights and noise—the people in the stands, the band, the cheerleaders.

Woooooow... Doooo youuu feeeeel it?

Yeeeeeeeaaaah . . .I . . . dooooooo . . . We were just grinning from ear to ear, sensing all this stuff going on all around the vicinity of our helmets.

The only bad part was actually playing the game.

When you're tripping on acid, you just want to watch things for a *looooong* time—which doesn't work well during a football game.

I was in my fullback position on offense and got called for a swing left pitch. Well, I got the route just fine, but I must have telegraphed my route really clearly to the opposition. Because by the time the slow-moving ball finally wobbled in its perfect, beautiful, purposeful arch towards my waiting, outstretched, welcoming, open hands and arms . . . I got absolutely crushed by three hungry defensemen.

I'm sure we lost that game—we were terrible, even when the players weren't stoned out of their minds.

≈

Incredibly, I graduated from high school a semester early, with barely passing grades. I don't even know how that happened, since I never went to class. But I managed to walk through the graduation ceremonies at Western High with all of my cronies, and had a great celebration. Yeah dude! I had Hawaiian leis stacked up on me, gifts from my mom and Auntie Ruthie and all their Hawaiian friends.

It was great to be out of high school. But I was having problems with the typical yelling and screaming and throwing things around the house. After a few months of being out of high school and still living at home, I just couldn't handle the tension in the house.

Just after the spring semester was over, I got into a fight with my dad over buying a car that he didn't approve of. So a few days later, I did the only thing I could do: I packed up and moved to Hawaii for the summer to take a break before starting college in the fall.

I lived with Uncle Clarence and his family for a few months, out in the country—horses, cows, pigs. Pretty cool. I worked with my uncle and his company, Concrete Coring Company, repairing the Honolulu Airport runway, then I moved out to my own place on the North Shore of Oahu, where all the surf action was. Got a job in a little market and surfed to my heart's content.

I really pushed myself to the edge on that trip. A local hotshot, James "Booby" Jones, had made the cover of *Surfer* magazine. Surfing as a competitive sport was really starting to take off. I wouldn't be competitive for a while yet, but I wanted in. One day I was at Waimea Bay, a famous big wave surf spot on the North Shore, waiting for my buddy to show up. Where was he?

The swell had jumped. It's odd to get a sizable north swell in springtime, but here it was.

And here *I* was, sitting at the beach watching it. It was a monster.

I told myself, *Dude, this is what you're here for—this is your heritage. If you don't go out, you're going to regret it forever.*

Life or death? Who cares!

I paddle out. The shore break is just a *monster,* very stressful. I make it through that and it's a little calmer paddling towards the channel, where the wave tapers off and the current pulls you out.

The waves keep getting bigger with each new set.

I'm out for an hour and still haven't caught a wave yet . . .

The crowd is pretty nutty, regulars all over the ocean: Bobby Owens, Booby Jones on his three redwood stringer Rhino Chaser, and a number of other nuts. "Nuts" because they'd get rolled by a massive wave and just come up laughing and joking. Meantime, I'm following the pack back and forth, trying to pick off my one wave just to get back in.

Finally, I catch my medium-size wave and ride it all the way, screaming and swooping and racing up and over and through the shore break. I'm pretty stoked to have gone out, but even more stoked to be back on the beach again.

Alive.

Taking off for Hawaii from December to the end of summer ended up being the best thing I could have done for myself at that time. I got a call from Mom about a month after I left. She said that Bill had gotten into it with my dad, who'd cracked him pretty good.

I was glad it wasn't me. It probably would've been if I'd stayed.

Chapter Eight

Even though we lived thirty miles apart, and in different worlds, I had gotten pretty tight with Nicole's friend Kris Kumer over the last couple of years. Kris was so beautiful—long, sun-bleached blond hair, large lungs, a full, pretty smile, and big blue eyes. As Nicole and I drifted apart, I fell for Kris and we started going out. Her parents didn't approve of me—I was from the wrong side of the tracks and all—but we were sixteen, and Kris and her parents didn't get along all that well anyway. Their opinion didn't matter much to either of us.

One night, Kris felt reckless and invited me to hang out with her and her friends at one of her parents' parties. Her parents' parties were nothing like the parties I had with my friends, but they still included drugs and alcohol—just a more refined variety. This particular party included a piano player who was inhaling amyl nitrite out of this weird metal inhaler.

We were taking hits with him in the backyard, getting all numb headed, just cracking up and partying all night.

I was tripping on watching all the high society types and fooling around with Kris, who looked amazing that night in a bright white, thigh-high dress. Eventually, probably inevitably, we got into pretty heavily groping and grappling under the bushes. Unfortunately, I made the mistake of bringing Kris back inside with grass stains—they were hard to miss on that little Spanish dress! Her mother was really pissed. Kris told me later that her mother actually backhanded her after I left. We laughed about it, as I recall.

But Kris and I continued to see each other all the time. She would come to my baseball games, and I would go to meet her at the beach, or at her job working part-time at Hobie Surf Shop. Sometimes she'd ride her bike to Newport Beach, where I would go to surf and to hang out with her.

Then she went off to school at USC. We saw each other a few times during those college years, but only once in a while. We both had our own lives to explore.

By 1977, I finally got tired of doing nothing but partying and surfing my brains out every day. I needed something more mentally stimulating. I was beginning to understand that there might be more to life, and that my ambition and drive could get me somewhere pretty good. I left high school with a GPA of something like 1.28, way down in the basement. But for some reason, almost as soon as I graduated, I realized that I wanted to do more with my life. I was still getting into fights, but I began to see how all my confidence and angry energy could work for me in ways that wouldn't get me in trouble.

Most of all, I guess, I wanted to do better than my dad and brother Billy. Fortunately, I had some better role models on Mom's side of the family. All of my mother's brothers had graduated high school and gone to college. They were doing really well in the world, so why not me?

I knew that if I wanted to make something of myself, I had to get educated, like my uncles. I decided to go to Orange Coast College. It wasn't hard to get in, even with my high school grades. OCC was a junior college in Costa Mesa, not far from the beach. It prided itself on being number one out of nine Orange County junior colleges in getting their graduates transferred to the University of California and Cal State systems. Boom! I was headed somewhere I'd never imagined I could go.

I buckled down and did really well at Orange Coast. Don't get me wrong, I didn't suddenly change personalities and turn into a grind. I always made time to party and keep up my surfing. But something must have just snapped into place, because for the first time ever, I focused on school first and surfing second.

Oh, I was on the surf team—of course! I used to make my own surfboards, ever since the days I was in a high school plastics class. I called them Hale's Home Grown, after my Hawaiian name, Hale. Each one had a big laminated pot leaf on the deck as my logo. With Kris off at USC, I had another girlfriend, Judy. I even put her name on my surfboard—I called it "Judy Baby." Judy and I went out for about half of the time I was at OCC.

I worked a couple of jobs to support myself, and moved in with some new friends I had met at school. My roommates, Jeff Carrillo and Scot Kelly, were both on the ski team, and literally forced me to join them. Between ski team and surf team, I had lots of friends to party with—and did, all the time.

But I also stressed about grades and homework, and pretty soon I had a 3.5 GPA.

Miraculous.

Brilliant times, those junior college years!

All too soon I could see the end of the two-year OCC program approaching, and I knew it was time to go to the next level. So I made an appointment with my guidance counselor, a guy named Chuck. But it turned out that old Chuck didn't really have my best interests in mind.

"Don't bother trying to get in to a UC school," he told me point blank after one look at me. "You don't have the necessary mental equipment."

Man! That was the wrong thing to tell me. It made my blood boil to have this pompous ass assume I was just some dumb airhead kid from the wrong side of the tracks. It just made me want to go to a UC school even more.

So I applied to *two* UC schools and a couple of the lower-tier state schools that I thought I might have a chance of getting into. And much to Chuck's surprise (and mine, too, I must admit) I *did* get accepted—by the University of California at Santa Barbara, no less. This was my dream school: a UC school, just a hundred miles north of Los Angeles, practically *on* the beach, and not far from home.

Wow!

The University of California wanted me.

"We are pleased to inform you of your admission to the Santa Barbara campus of the University of California for the Fall 1979 quarter. . . . "

I sat on my bed reading that letter over and over and over. It was incredible! *Maybe I could actually achieve something worthwhile.* UCSB was just a whole other level of goodness. I could feel it: this was a real turning point in my life.

And it turned out to be just that.

My first week at UCSB, I went to the surf team meeting. The coach invited me for a surf after class the next day, at a secret spot. Nice guy! When I stopped by his house so he could take me there, he offered me a little seedy cookie. Turned out to be a magic mushroom cookie—which I only figured it when I found myself staring at the kelp in the water and not doing much surfing. I look up, and my coach has a big smile on his face.

Ahhhh . . . Welcome to UCSB. So happy!

Billy came north a couple of times to hang with me at UCSB. For a while, it looked like he might be on a better track too. He got some full-time work outside the family paving company, which allowed him to get out from under Dad's relentless criticism about his neglectful, irresponsible, and disrespectful attitude.

Working more also afforded my brother the opportunity to acquire some nice new toys—motorcycles, cars, and girls chief among them. For Billy, this was a real step up from breaking into houses and getting busted.

But the one element of Billy's old lifestyle that didn't get left out of this new, more productive one was the drugs. Billy was smart, good-looking, athletic, a wild storyteller, and a hard worker—when he was sober. But no matter how busy he stayed with work or how much fun he was having trying to carve out his own path in life, the drugs were always calling him.

He began getting deeper and deeper into serious drugs—meth, heroin, crack. Speedballs were one of his favorites. He'd mix coke with heroin and shoot the whole thing at once—the same mixture that killed John Belushi in 1982. Sometimes he'd freebase coke and smoke it out of a big glass pipe. I would get calls from Mom, from his girlfriend, his friends—and sometimes even from Billy himself—to please help! I'd have to leave school and deal with whatever shit he was up to, get him out of jail, try to help him unwind it somehow.

One time I had to talk Bill down from a scary haunted house episode. When I showed up to calm him down at his freezing cold house, he was hallucinating, overdosing on a few different drugs, and threatening to kill his roommates for telling "the Devil" to come after him. There are literally too many stories like this to tell, and the end is always the same—not too long after I rescue him, I get another call to rescue him.

What happened to make Billy like this?

Even as a little kid, he was a wild man. His unsettling behavior would make any parent worry about his sanity. Was my brother born with this frenetic disposition, unable to be soothed by mother's milk or to ever achieve a deep, comforting, sound sleep? Maybe. I know my dad's attitude didn't help.

Who was the egg and who was the chicken when it came to the antagonism between my dad and my brother?

I was never quite sure. Did my dad's early neglect and abuse push Billy to always steer left instead of right? Did a constant diet of Dad's disapproval and impatience breed the mental and emotional instability that drove my brother to flip through life's events like a casual reshuffle of the cards he was dealt?

Maybe it was a bad combination of genes and Dad.

Hell, it doesn't take a genius to sort out most early-stage psychological issues. In most cases, you can just talk to a person for a couple of hours and the stories will come spilling out. It's not as though Billy didn't ask for help, in his own over-the-top way. Therapists call what he did—the drugs, the criminal activity, the wild and crazy stunts—"acting out," a cry for help. Billy has certainly acted out over the years!

Hmmm! Do you think he just might have an issue with trust, self-confidence, self-esteem, insecurity, or fear? Do you think it stems from neglect, abuse, mental or physical abandonment, maybe through something biological and inborn? Is there something I'm missing?

I could go on trying to figure out what went wrong, and over the years I have, too many times. But why? For what purpose? It's too late to point fingers; the damage was done a long time ago. Despite his best efforts to the contrary, Billy is still alive. Despite all the acting out, Mom and I are still saving him from himself, and we still love the crazy bastard.

❧

It's amazing how much I crammed into life in those days. I always had part-time jobs and worked hard at my classes, but I seemed to have plenty of time for a lot of other things, including surfing, partying, and girls.

For most of my time at UCSB I had a doll of a girlfriend, Kristen Hodgins. Poor girl! I was a madman then—in a frat, on the surf team, had tons of nutty friends always doing nutty things, but she stuck by me through all of it. I thought I would end up marrying her, and I'm pretty sure she expected it as well. She couldn't have been a better, more fun girlfriend.

I loved her to death, I really did. But I truly loved to surf and party too!

I surfed extremely well, especially in contests—not because I was better than everyone else, but because I understood how to compete and did whatever was necessary to win. I was the top kid in our The National Scholastic Surfing Association (NSSA) league at Santa Barbara, and we ended up winning the league title for UCSB, their first league championship ever. Yeah, I was pretty stoked!

NSSA had its biggest Summer National competition at Huntington Beach each year. All the best amateur surfers were in it. I did pretty well and advanced into the final heat of the contest.

Well, I advanced for about ten minutes.

Then one of the organizers found me and explained that there had been a recount and I had been edged out by a half a point—so sorry, so sorry.

Fuck!

Still, I was pretty mellow considering that it was only the biggest amateur surf contest in the nation—or the world, for that matter. I ended up eighth overall. The cool thing was that the same guy, Chuck Allen, called and told me to make sure I showed up to the awards ceremony. I was kind of clueless, and thought that he was just being nice.

But I showed up for the ceremony with my good buddy Steve Whitaker as my date. We got so stoned beforehand that I barely took in the news: When they announced the new 1980 team, I was on it.

What? I thought I had no chance of making the team, but I got selected—and not as an alternate.

Ron McElroy! On the team.

I was so stoked, I high-fived every single person in the place. I had a smile from ear to ear the whole night.

In early August of 1980, the National Scholastic Surfing Association team, with me on it, got invited to the International Board Riding Teams Challenge to face off against the Australian SLSA team in Australia.

We landed in Sydney and drove to a town called Surfers Paradise. That was the actual name of the suburb on the Gold Coast in Queensland. There couldn't have been a more appropriate location for this contest. And we were there for two weeks!

It was cool seeing the Australian countryside, stopping in our big white-and-blue bus at surf breaks or little meat pie shops. We were taken to all these prearranged ceremonies, functions, and promotions—we felt like celebrities. And once again, I was on a surf trip with my buddy Steve Whitaker.

The locals had agreed to house us, and Steve and I were placed with a family that had two really cool kids our age: Roland, the crazy son, and Louise, the absolute firing daughter, whom I was delighted to hang with without much delay. She was hot! They took us around everywhere with their local friends.

We had surfing competitions all day, and then functions or parties at night. We hung out with some legendary guys, like Neville Hyman—a big surfboard shaper of the time and Michael Peterson's buddy John, a promotion guy from the local radio station. The stories of Michael are just insanely off the charts. He was arguably the best surfer Australia has ever produced. But eventually he just lost it all to drugs.

In those days, Burleigh Heads was known for its six-foot barrel waves, but on this trip the conditions were sloppy three- or four-footers. Oh well. We surfed anyway! My most important heat was just me against one opponent, a guy named Geoff Dews. I knew that Dews was the better man. So—competitor that I am—I got an interference called against him.

Here's how it works to get an interference: If you're closer to the peak (the breaking part of the wave), you have the right of way. If the other guy takes off on you, no matter how far away he is, it's interference, and he gets his highest-scoring wave deducted from his total. So I tricked Dews into thinking that I wasn't going to take this wave, laying back until the very last minute. He thought I wasn't going to take it at all and started out himself. But a split second later I did take the wave—and it looked as if he had stolen my right of way.

Bad on him, as the Aussies say. The judges ruled an interference, and I won.

I felt a bit like a schmuck. But I won the heat and helped get the team in a tiebreaker, sudden-death surf-off between the two best guys surfing: Marty Hoffman and the Australian Bryce Ellis. In the end, though, the Aussies edged us out and won the competition.

Oh well. As Bill Bolman, president of the International Professional Surfers Association said as he presented the award, "There were no losers—you both won—surf was the winner."

We all partied anyway. Great trip!

Louise and I kept in touch after I got back to America. She wrote me a lot, and seemed to be taking our relationship a lot more seriously than I did. But I didn't really think about it until she showed up on my doorstep in Santa Barbara. She stayed with me for quite a while. I was pretty clueless. I had no idea that she wanted a long-term thing, maybe even marriage. It was a bit awkward when I had to break it off, especially since I didn't know it was on. Duh!

I wasn't ready for anything serious at that point, even if the girl was.

Now that I was getting famous, at least in my own mind, I was starting to enjoy having been recruited and inducted into the Santa Barbara chapter of the legendary Sigma Chi fraternity—no small thing. It was a really old national fraternity with famous members all over the country. But it wasn't stodgy. I thought I'd seen a lot of wild partying, but Sigma Chi exposed me to a whole new level of utter lunacy, some of it looking pretty insane from the perspective of the older guy I am now.

I watched guys launch Molotov cocktails with balloon catapults.

I saw pledges forced to drink flamers in the dark (start by pouring a Bacardi 151 shooter, and then light it on fire) and then spit them out, which lit their faces on fire.

I also saw pledges forced to wear a gas mask hooked up to a bong that pumped weed into their lungs with a motor, filling the facepiece until they were choking.

One time a brother had a plate of spaghetti smashed on his face, knocking out two of his front teeth. . . . And on and on.

At one point—not too surprising, I guess—we were put on probation and almost kicked off campus.

Holy macaroni!

I figured that this was just college life.

I kept in touch with home and everything seemed like it was going better there, too. Dad was still sober, and his business was doing great. He bought a few different blocks of property, five to ten acres each, with three or four horses and a new prefab house, barn, corral—the whole works.

That was right before he went off into the desert to walk backwards and bury his money. Go figure!

Eventually, despite some moments of lucid sobriety, my dad lost most of his mind and his money. At the end of his life he only had his Social Security and veteran's benefits, enough to pay rent and groceries. I helped him with the rent and extras when he needed it. But I think my Dad was just tired and disillusioned with life, and sensed that the end was near. By this time Mom had moved out. But even though they were living separately, she'd look in on him on a regular basis to make sure he was relatively OK.

∿

I wound up majoring in law and society at UCSB, thinking maybe I would go on to law school. But even though I never did, it taught me a lot about a lot of things that have helped me to be successful in all the businesses I have gotten into in my life. Studying criminal justice taught me discipline, and the coursework in general gave me a social, psychological, and philosophical grounding that has served me well through the years. *Out-think your adversaries* is what I learned then, and I've tried to do that ever since!

As it happened, I barely made it through my last class. I had taken off winter quarter of 1982 to compete in a series of big pro surfing competitions, and only came back at the last minute to finish my thesis by the skin of my teeth. My thesis advisor, Ms. Binion, had the kindness and understanding to let me get away with it. She gave me a passing grade when I know my thesis absolutely sucked.

Thank you for letting me graduate, Ms. Binion!

After graduation, it took me a while to comprehend the fact that school was over, that it was time to get a job and move on. I hadn't done interviews or internships like everyone else. I just hadn't given it a thought—too busy being in the UCSB moment!

But it was all too clear that I needed a real job. The natural place to go was my surfing sponsors. Off-Shore Clothing had been one of my sponsors when I was competing all over California, Central America, Hawaii, and Australia. I went to see them and persuaded them to let me rep their Team Hard-Core surf-wear line. As a West Coast salesman from Santa Barbara to Stinson Beach, near San Francisco, I got to work and surf meet cool people at all the surf shops where I lived and up north, too. It was sweet: work, surf, work, surf.

Great job. But not enough money.

My days at UCSB had taught me how to have crazy fun, but also that I truly could achieve my goals. I just need to know what they were.

Right now, I knew two things: I wanted more dough and a bigger potential for the future. I talked about it to everyone I knew, hoping for some direction. Al Merrick, who supplied my surfboards at the time and was pretty much the guru of surfboard design and manufacturing, encouraged me to go pro. He pointed out that I had a good chance in pro surfing, which could lead to championship prize money.

So I decided to go for it. I told myself that if I didn't do extremely well in a short period of time, then I was going to have to get a real job.

I did a few contests, and brought home a few bucks from smaller events, which helped my confidence. Then I went for the biggest venue of the year, the World Cup at Sunset Beach, Hawaii.

I killed it in the trials rounds. But on the third day the swell had jumped from overhead size to triple overhead, heaving surf. Guys were calling it "fifteen feet Hawaiian," which means *seriously big waves.* My big boards weren't as dialed-in as they should have been, and I hadn't spent a lot of time in surf that size. I finished in the middle of my heat—not high enough to advance.

I was bummed, and I knew I had to make a choice. Stick it out against a whole new level of top rate professional surfers, or face reality, get to work, and make something of myself. Not a tough call at the time. I decided to cut my losses and move on.

Sometimes, looking back, I wish I had stuck with surfing a little while longer and really pushed it as far as I could. But I was getting older, and knew I had to have something more solid and long-term.

So I looked around to see where there was money to be made. Let's see . . . what was hot in Southern California besides beaches, surfing, girls, drugs, and music?

Real estate.

I had a good instinct for property, even in those days. All over Southern California, a lot of farms and low-cost housing were being bulldozed and developed to make way for more expensive housing and industry. A lot of guys I had known from UC Santa Barbara were making big bucks buying and selling real estate for clients. Even my dad, when he was sober, had an instinct for buying property. So it made sense to me that I could do it, too. I decided to set my sights on commercial real estate.

There was just one problem.

In late 1982, at the tender age of twenty-five, I didn't interview very well—to put it mildly. I was still saying things like *Rad, dude!* or *Killer building!* No surprise (except to me), that all the big brokerage houses turned me down for employment. I got the message: I had to polish up my act.

A few kind people recommended, very diplomatically, that I should get some seasoning, some experience at selling. "Go work for Xerox or Panasonic or Sharp," said one guy, "and then come back and talk to us."

I took his advice to the letter. I put on my suit and tie and sold photocopiers for exactly one year to the day. In the beginning, it was a shock to my system. I couldn't believe that people selling copiers actually worked eight hours straight, every single day.

But pretty soon I realized that I was speaking less like a surf bum and more like everyone else. I began to dress better and have better manners. I learned to listen attentively—a key skill if you want to get anywhere in sales. Most important, I learned how to close the deal, do all the paperwork, get the order, pocket the money, and move on to the next customer.

To this day, selling copiers is still the worst job I've ever had. I hated it. But it was a means to an end, so I did it. And I got used to it. And then I got really good at it. I sold a lot of copiers.

∼

In 1983, fresh out of the copier-sales mill, I finally got what I consider my first real job. I went to work for the Charles Dunn Company, a national commercial real estate firm, in Los Angeles. I was in training to sell office buildings, lease office space, and all the rest. I loved that job! I dressed up, paid attention, listened, learned what they were doing, buckled down, and kicked butt. I worked my ass off, and pretty soon I started to make real money.

I was the crazy kid that cold-called like a madman. I just loved the business. In at six a.m.; hard at work until six p.m. Day in, day out. I did well and kept making my numbers, and got plenty of top-performer awards—including free trips to Hawaii. What could be more perfect?

~

When I began selling copiers, I'd started to keep company with Kris Kumer again. We dated pretty steadily and just kept it up as I was getting my start in the real estate business.

When I was started doing better financially, Kris began to appreciate that I was done with the crazy life. I was going to behave myself and settle down, make a living, have some dough, be a success.

She began talking about marriage.

Chapter Nine

Those top-performer trips to Hawaii were like a continuation of the life I'd always known. During high school and college, and afterwards as a pro surfer, I'd made regular trips back to Hawaii to visit with my mother's family and get in as much surfing and crazy fun on the beach as possible.

Most Americans only get to see the public side of Hawaii, reserved for tourists. But I've been lucky enough to learn about the Hawaiian culture from the inside out. Mom's family members who remained in the islands number in the hundreds. With this unique perspective, I've been able to understand Hawaii's alluring beauty and spirit, but I've also witnessed an ongoing struggle as the island state wrestles with its identity.

On one hand, Hawaii is economically subservient to the tourist industry. Without the millions of tourists who come for their vacations, unemployment would be rampant. This means that the local population is dependent on dressing the part—beautiful hula girls, native drummers, hotel luaus, and all the rest—to promote the glorification of Hawaii's ancient culture that so many pay to see year in and year out.

Many Hawaiians struggle with this dependency, viewing it as a necessary evil, taking the bad along with the good. And a good percentage of the population is happy to have gainful employment. But underneath there is a constant, simmering resentment toward the "*haole* from the mainland." This resentment has been there as long as I can remember.

The concept of a sovereign Hawaii has been talked about for decades, fueled by the constant siege by American corporate interests, determined to squeeze every last drop of profit from an ever-shrinking genuine Hawaii. The simple ancient way of life still exists beneath the shadow of the mainlanders' dreams of high-rise resorts, expansive golf courses, and increased real estate prices, but it's harder and harder to find. Since my first visit in 1965, the changes have been sad, disturbing, and unmistakable.

Recent overtures in the form of low-paying menial employment opportunities were meant to placate the struggling native Hawaiian population, but have only exacerbated an already seething resentment. My cousins, aunts, and uncles complained bitterly that their state was being stolen: too many *haoles,* no respect, crowded surf, increased housing costs, the slaughter of the Hawaiian way of life.

These arguments are by no means unwarranted. But would it really be better to go back to old Hawaii? We know that will never happen. We already have government programs to give property back to the indigenous population, but those are far from perfect. Waiting lists are backlogged. Thousands of full-blood Hawaiians can't qualify financially to accept the minimum ongoing obligations of property ownership.

And benefits like the Hawaiians-only schools are being challenged as discriminating against non-Hawaiian residents.

Here lies the dilemma: are we a strong, self-sufficient warrior nation like our ancestors, or are we a whipped huddle of dependent stepchildren conveniently coerced into Uncle Sam's sprawling American smorgasbord?

Passing time has dulled the fervor surrounding Hawaii's tarnished history—the manner in which the islands were annexed has resurfaced in the Hawaiian subconscious as a reluctant acceptance of their ill-gotten fate. Right or wrong, this self-perception is nevertheless very real and present in a large segment of the Hawaiian psyche. Yes, some Hawaiians accept their oppressed status with good-humored resignation, but a significant number just can't hack it.

These men and women have chosen to escape life's daily confrontational subjections via numbing intoxication: marijuana and alcohol, sure, but most and worst of all speed, ice, crystal meth—the most addictive drug ever produced.

I'd guess that 50 percent of Hawaiian youth have tried and a fair percentage of are hooked on this malignant elixir. The level of addiction is difficult to estimate. I have seen firsthand how this drug can drift through the portals of every human sensory connection, rendering its victim senseless.

～

Escaping the hustle-bustle of Southern California to rest up in Maui several years back, I saw an example of this mind-boggling destruction. On the way to our modest little plantation-style house just outside Paia, we noticed some action around a car parked in the middle of the road. I went to see what was going on.

A pretty Hawaiian girl was slumped over the steering wheel of a brand-new yellow and white Cadillac with half her head blown off. A shocking, horrible, bloody mess. She couldn't have been much more than twenty years old. It was awful and heartbreaking to look at.

The folks out in the street told us she was a local girl. She'd been on ice for days, and this morning she'd stolen this car right off the lot after taking it on a test drive. She sped off, leaving the car salesmen standing in the dust. He called the cops, and half a dozen flashing blue-and-whites took off after her in a high-speed pursuit, whizzing recklessly by pedestrians strolling along the narrow streets of the restored sugar mill town.

The Caddie then turned straight up the main street, already blocked off by a couple more flashing blue-and-whites that had arrived on the scene from the opposite direction. Guns were drawn, and the police issued their commands loud and clear. But instead of stopping or giving up, the girl made a sharp U-turn, ending up half on the curb and half in the street, surrounded by scared cops with weapons. She shifted into reverse and floored the gas pedal, heading directly at one of the officers. All weapons were discharged.

So many fatal shots were fired no one knew exactly which cop's bullets had hit her. She was pronounced dead on the scene.

I later found out that this same girl had been responsible for multiple robberies throughout the small community. Bold daylight incursions—she simply walked in and took anything from cash to articles that could be easily pawned for a fraction of their real value. She needed cash to score the ice and stave off the downside of coming off crystal meth.

Everyone was shocked, including the police. It was sad, puzzling, and horrible. It had happened right next door, but it was a million miles away from the illusory world of waving palm trees and ukuleles at the beachfront hotels.

I was flattered that a nice girl like Kris Kumer thought she and I should be married, even if her parents still kind of looked down on me. I had mixed feelings about getting married and I didn't know if I was ready to have kids, either, which I knew was on Kris's mind.

It somehow all happened, but it took two tries. And if Kris's parents didn't hate me already, I gave them good reason.

One year before we were finally married, we had gotten officially engaged and announced we would get married right away. Her mom and dad got everything ready for a big, gala wedding, five hundred guests, in their hometown of San Marino, next door to Pasadena. Maybe I really wasn't ready. In my mind, the wedding seemed to be all about them: their friends, and how they thought things like this should be done. I couldn't take all the stress and fuss, the complaining and fighting about every little detail.

So two weeks before The Big Day, I called off the wedding. Kris's parents had to cancel the flowers, the cake, music, everything. They had to tell their hundreds of guests that their daughter's big wedding was off. They were extremely pissed off, to say the least, and I was on their bad person list for years after. Kris was devastated, mad, and embarrassed. I didn't think I would ever see her again.

Nevertheless, we stayed together, and a year later, we managed to get married in a way that felt more natural—to me, anyway. We eloped and went to my Uncle Bill's Jesus Coming Soon church in Honolulu. It was a cool, low-key Hawaiian wedding ceremony with leis and local blessings. Uncle Ronnie was there, with several other of my Hawaiian relatives. And Kris's really good friend, Morjonn, and her husband just happened to be on our flight. They witnessed the wedding for us and partied with us that night.

My Uncle Pastor Bill wasn't crazy about the idea of us eloping, but he married us anyway—with strict commands to ask for God's forgiveness for not having all of our family present. He even got us the *kamaina* rate (the local Hawaiian discount) on our hotel in Waikiki. I love that about my Hawaiian family: they'll do just about anything for you anytime.

My mom was disappointed that we did it the way we did, and that she wasn't there to see the wedding. But she was happy we were back together. And we'd gotten married at Jesus Coming Soon church, so how could it possibly be a bad thing?

Kris was just really happy to finally get married. She didn't care if no one in her family approved of what she was doing. Eventually, her parents caved and threw a big, formal shindig a few months later, back at their house in Monarch Beach.

And just like that, Kris was ready to have a family.

I was kind of afraid to have kids—coming from my family, I think that's understandable! But Kris really wanted them, and she had a physical condition that meant she had to have kids right away or it would be harder as she got older. By the time we'd been married six months she was pregnant, and William Brett McElroy was born on February 15, 1986.

The birth of my son turned out to be the best experience I had ever imagined. It was great to be a father!

Our second son, John Cameron McElroy, was born on February 23, 1988. I still loved being a dad—that feeling has never left me. But after she gave birth to Cameron, Kris and I started to have some problems and not seeing eye-to-eye on everything.

She began to seem stressed all the time, really fricken angry at me, and I couldn't figure out why. It was all the time, no letup. She said that she had postpartum depression. I knew she was superbusy—two little boys, and moving into our first new house right after she gave birth. And she had to deal with continual disapproval from her parents about their son-in-law. They didn't like how I looked, and they didn't appreciate my general personality or behavior.

I tried to figure out what to do. Maybe I was drinking too much—Kris felt that I had "alcoholic tendencies." So I quit drinking for a year. But the next Christmas we went to my friends' house for a party, and they bought me nonalcoholic beer so I could at least join the festivities with everyone else! Then they decided to play a little trick. When they were getting my drinks for me, they emptied out the nonalcoholic beer and filled those bottles up with real beer. Lighthearted fun, right? Well, Kris suspected I was cheating on my no-alcohol vows since I was a little too jovial, smelled like booze, and went to bed early all of a sudden.

The next morning, the proverbial shit hit the fan. Things were definitely not getting better between us. I couldn't seem to get anything right where Kris was concerned.

In 1990, when I was thirty-two, my father died, just three months after he'd been diagnosed with lung cancer. My son Brett, about four years old at the time, had come with me to take Dad out to lunch and then over to the Veterans Hospital for chemo. I knew Dad was having a hard time; that was evident. I saw the pain on his face when we dropped him off, even though he was trying hard to hide it.

I knew Dad was living on borrowed time. The doctors had made it crystal clear that he could pass any day, week, or month. I tried to prepare myself to accept this cold fact. I spent as much time as I could with him, trying to show him that someone cared that his time was limited. He never confirmed it in so many words, but he seemed to know how I felt.

Still, the reality that he was going to die never really sunk in.

About two days later, a voice on the phone told me that my dad was dead. This guy, a neighbor, I guess, had found his body on the floor.

It was like a punch in the gut.

I was shocked at how deep my sorrow was. I couldn't believe it. How could I grow up resenting someone so much and yet be this traumatized by his death? How could

I have mastered a stone-cool response to every emotional circumstance with steely perfection, only to lose complete control now?

I drove the hour to his place in pouring rain, sobbing the entire way. I gathered enough control to stop at a liquor store to pick up a bottle of Seagram's Seven, a twelve-pack of tall Budweiser cans, and a pack of Camels. I was now fully supplied to pay my respects to Dad with all of his favorites.

I don't know exactly what I was thinking when I got there. Since I didn't have a key, I wiped my face with my sleeve, pulled it over my hand for protection, and punched out a glass section in his front door. I reached through, released the lock, and walked inside, just staring around.

Then a very scared looking man came to the door from inside the house and turned a flashlight in my face.

"What are you doing?" he said.

He's the voice from the phone, I thought.

"I'm Bill's son. I talked to you on the phone. I just want to be here for a little while."

"What about the window?? he asked, sheepishly. *Must be the landlord.*

"Sorry. But don't worry, I'll pay for it."

He left me alone with memories of my dad. I saw remnants of where he had passed on the tile floor of the kitchen; a tuft of hair, a spot of blood. I stared again for a long while.

Then I lit a smoke, took a big drag.

I cracked open the Seagram's, took a big swig.

Took a couple more and kept staring. . . .

The next thing I knew, bright sunlight pierced my eyes, making me squint and waking me up. I rubbed my eyes and realized I had a crushing headache. I was lying on the floor of an empty living room littered with empty beer cans, an empty bottle of Seagram's, and cigarette butts everywhere.

Confused, I looked around, and slowly remembered where I was.

I saw my dad's old paintings propped up on the floor, against the wall, surrounding me. He had never really stopped painting, all his life. I couldn't remember it that morning, but I must have collected them from around his small cottage and set them up during my all-night grief session. They were all portraits—Mother Teresa, Oliver North, General Patton, a self-portrait. . . . Now they were all staring at me.

I guess I wasn't taking my dad's passing as well as I thought I would.

If I had a dime for every person, professional and not, who recommended that I forget about his death and move on, yeah, I'd have a few bucks. I felt his presence for years. I conquered a lot of emotional problems during this period of time, always thinking with his now-superior guidance. Solving personal issues, including letting go, something I could understand only by experiencing the traumatic death of a loved one. So, strange as it may seem, I'll forever be grateful to my dad for what I learned from him after he passed away.

～

I had to handle Dad's death alone. No one else was around—brother Billy was medicated, sister Susie was off in cult-land, and Mom was visiting relatives in Hawaii when he died.

It was surreal. Going to the morgue to identify his body, ordering a coffin, being asked what accessories he preferred . . . it was like buying an overpriced car. I remember the dank smell of that funeral home; it hung on you like a wet rag. Dealing with death is just a terrible experience.

Kris was pretty unsympathetic about the whole thing. She insisted that I pull it together and cremate the body because it was easier and cheaper.

I didn't have the nerve to call my mom to break the news to her while she was away, so I called her brother, Pastor Bill, to get his opinion. He said what I already knew—their Christian faith called for a proper burial, allowing the body to rest in peace and the soul to rise to heaven.

"Forget cremation," I told Kris. She started on a tirade about it not being our responsibility to take care of my father's death, emotionally or financially.

At that moment I knew that the love between us was dead and the marriage was over.

Kris and I separated, but we kept seeing each other, especially when I was spending time with the boys. We both calmed down a little, counted to ten, and after six months I moved back in.

For a while, things got better. Then they went sideways again.

I remember sitting on the front porch one sunny day. Kris was weeding, and I was relaxing after playing basketball with the boys. Suddenly, out of nowhere, she told me that she wanted to have a girl.

I was shocked. I'm thinking, *How can we take the stress of a new baby. Sounds like a dangerous idea at this point. So don't just give in like you always do. If this marriage is going to work from now on, you have to speak your piece.* So I did.

"We just got back together," I told her. "Can't we take it one step at a time then talk later?"

"No. I want an answer now or else I want a divorce."

Bam. Wow. That was it, the line in the sand. I managed to say nothing hasty, but was determined not to give in again.

I went to see my shrink, Bruce Parsons. Kris and I had been going to a marriage counselor for some time, but she suggested that I have my own therapist to deal with my addiction problems. Bruce was a recovering alcoholic himself, with lots of war stories about his years as a boozer and junkie. Sometimes I felt like I was the therapist just listening to his problems.

When I told him that Kris was demanding that I agree to have a girl or she'd leave me, he said, "Do you love her?"

"No."

I was shocked to hear myself say this, but that was my gut feeling, my honest answer.

"But I don't want to lose my boys, so I'm afraid to get divorced."

"Not a good reason to stay married," he said, shaking his head. "It won't work, and eventually you'll get divorced whether you want to or not."

He was right.

I stayed, however. It was a dumb thing to do but I did it. I told her I didn't want another kid. And then, sure enough, she actually divorced me.

Maybe she thought her parents would like it if she divorced me, since to this day she still struggles to get their approval. They had always told her to stay employable, because she'd be divorced someday. Well, their prophecy came true, thanks in great part to Kris herself.

She's never remarried, and now they give her grief for divorcing me way back in the day, when they were part of the reason. Crazy!

I didn't lose the boys. I see them regularly on weekends, holidays, and over the summer. And Kris and I got together frequently to talk about them, compare notes, discuss stuff like school, money, how they were going through changes. We still do.

During one of those get-togethers not that long ago, Kris told me that the real reason she divorced me wasn't because she wanted another kid. That was just an excuse. It was because I was having an affair.

What?

I was shocked. I had no idea what she was talking about. While we were still married and having a hard time, she said, she got a phone call from some girl saying that she loved me and wanted to marry me and that I was going to leave Kris any second.

Kris never said a word to me about it at the time. She just hated my guts and showed it every chance she could.

"How could you have believed some random phone call and not even given one thought to it being garbage?"

And garbage was really what it was. I had never heard of this other woman before, and never had any affair before Kris and I were separated. I was such an old-school guy. Naive or not, I've always felt like marriage makes things different. I was never unfaithful and lived monogamously the whole time Kris and I were together.

Chapter Ten

After I moved out of the house Kris and I had, there were two separate parts to my world: public and personal.

I kept making money, but my personal life was very stressful. After a while—separating, getting back together, trying to have quality time with the kids without going to war with their mother—it got to be too much. My business life began to suffer. Then suddenly I'm divorced, and just reeling.

What the hell happened to my great life? No more nice house, no more playing with the boys every day, no more visit-the-school night, not such a pillar of the community anymore. It all went sour with a snap of the fingers!

But I knew that Brett and Cameron were depending on me. And I was now paying alimony to Kris. I got a new job, with Grubb and Ellis Company, and things began to turn around.

I take after my mom. She taught me to just forget all the bad stuff and keep going, no matter what. Keep trying.

Keep up the steam and hold on to your daily routine. Keep bringing in the bucks. And I did.

By 1992, I had enough money and felt I was good enough at what I did to start my first company: Real Estate Management Corporation—REMC.

And on the private side, my luck held, and in 1993, I met Elizabeth.

～

After my divorce from Kris, I had dated a couple of psycho/stalker types. You know, the type of girl who calls and then hangs up, leaves poison pen notes in your mailbox, or sends you a black hand. For about a year-and-a-half, things were pretty dismal in that department.

Then one afternoon, I went into Hobie Surf Shop in Corona Del Mar with my boys to get some surf wax and check out some surfboards. Cameron and Brett were about four and six at that time, and pretty active. The girl who worked there was really sweet with them, even though they were running in and out of all the clothes and up and down the aisles, screaming and laughing. I thought that was a pretty noble personality trait, and I took a closer look. She had a name tag that said "Liz."

Very cool-looking girl, I thought. She must appreciate family. I introduced myself.

"Liz…I'm Ron. Pleased to meet you—and thanks for your patience."

I went back there a few times.

Well, the third or fourth time I went in, I bought a pair of trunks for Brett to go swimming at the club, which was our next stop. I had a Big Game hat on from the Cal-Stanford game, which I had been to recently.

She asked me about the game, and I told her I was a UC guy. She told me that she had gone to Menlo-Atherton High School on the San Francisco Peninsula and always went to Stanford games.

We talked, smiled, talked, smiled, talked . . . and the kids ran around the store some more. . . . But we were both oblivious to them for those few minutes. We were both in something of an altered state, I guess, and Liz forgot to remove the theft protection device from the trunks. It actually didn't go off when we left, and I only noticed it was still attached to the trunks when I put them on Brett at the club.

Great! Perfect excuse to go back to Hobie.

After our swim, back to see Liz, who was shocked that the buzzer hadn't gone off. As she was removing it, I took a shot.

"Would you like to do something one of these days?" I said.

Turned out that would be kind of hard.

"I would but I'm leaving for Austria in three days on this foreign studies program. It's a junior year overseas program."

Now, I'm not the typical guy with all the quick lines. But for some reason this flat-out lie came out of my mouth.

"Oh, really? That's wild! I'm supposed to go to France on business in a few months. How about I swing over to Austria while I'm there and visit?"

I'm sure she was thinking, *ax murderer!* But she gave me her phone number, probably figuring I'd never call, and we said good-bye.

But I did call. Right before she left for Austria, I called her up and we talked for two hours. Now normally, I despise talking on the phone. I have to really like someone to spend that kind of time on the phone. Clearly, I was far gone.

Liz left, and I got really busy at work, building up my sales at Grubb and Ellis. I never stopped thinking about her, though. So for three months—and this was way before email—we sent letters back and forth every couple of days. I think she saved all of hers. I sent her funny gifts, like Peterbilt hats for her and her card-playing friends, since she said they all "played like truckers."

Then, when I felt I could take a long-overdue vacation break from the office, I called her overseas. It was hard to talk on the phone, since she was an exchange student living with a family. But they actually loved the fact that Liz had this long-distance romance going on and were very courteous and happy when I called.

"I'll meet you in Munich and we'll drive to Innsbruck for the start of our ski trip," I told her, nearly screaming into the mouthpiece. Man, I was so pumped to fly over to see her, I couldn't wait.

And I finally fessed up: "I don't really have any business in France. I'm coming all the way over to Austria to have my first date with you." So I bought my ticket to Austria. Diving in, head first!

Lots of apprehension on both sides of the Atlantic once that was done.

We were pretty stoked, but a little freaked at the same time. I prepared, though. I had to bring some herb, since I'd heard that all they have in that region is hash. I had five big bombers rolled up in my Marlboro box. I figured I could just toss it if I needed to. No TSA X-raying you back then.

I got on the plane nervous as a cat. I'd started smoking cigarettes the day my dad died of lung cancer, so I'm sitting in the smoking section. (They still had that back then. The whole back four rows of the plane was filled with smoke.)

Wow, here we go. Off to Munich!

Hope Liz is there when I arrive.

❧

Uh-oh . . .

I'm staring out the window as we land in *München*, which is how they announce it. Early morning, and it looks *so cold* out there. I'm a knucklehead when I travel to cold places, thinking I can maintain my Hawaiian thing wherever I am. I had just returned from taking clients to Mexico for a fishing trip for a few days, so I'm sporting a drug dealer tan, slicked-back hair, white Mexican wedding shirt, jeans, and flip flops. Yeah, like that'll work in this climate.

We land and unload. Before picking up my stuff from the baggage area, I walk straight to the glass exit door to see if Liz is actually there.

I don't see her.

I head back to grab my duffle and notice a woman staring at me. I head back to the exit doors and that same lady is standing right in front them, so I can't go through. She's staring right at me, eyeball to eyeball, our contact direct. She says something in German. I'm thinking, *Gee, women are pretty aggressive here in Munich.* Then she whips out a badge and says, "Customs, come with me!"

Oh, shit! I glance back through the glass doors as she leads me to this little room behind the carousel. Still no Liz.

"Why are you here? Who are you here to see? Where are you travelling from?"

All these questions, and nothing is registering in my brain. I remember thinking, *You'd better answer these questions or you're screwed! C'mon do it, do it, . . .*

"I'm just coming here to ski with a friend. Probably be here for a week."

I never flinched, never removed my stare from hers. She caved a little.

"Do you have anything you shouldn't have?"

"No, Ma'am," I said, still looking right in her eyes.

Then she smiled and said, "Okay, you're free to go!"

I tried not to look too shocked, grabbed my duffle, turned, and began walking away. *Oh, man,* I thought, *damn, that Marlboro box. . . . Her hand is going to land on my shoulder any second. . . .* But it never did.

And then I saw Liz standing at the glass exit doors. She looked nervous, but happy to see me. All right! I grabbed her arm and whisked her toward the baggage carousel.

"I'm so glad to see you, but let's get out of this area," I said. *Oh my God, how exciting is this!* Two slightly nervous but really excited wannabe lovers seeing if this is really real. We jump in her rental car—a white BMW 320i, at my request, a great little car for the unlimited speed of the Autobahn. We're off to Innsbruck in style.

Along the way we stopped at little bars to grab a bite, drinking beer and having great talks. I was blown away by the Austrian landscape. Lots of homes somehow built at the peak of a steep, steep mountain—a beautiful, awe-inspiring landscape. When we got to our quaint little hotel in Innsbruck, we opened the door to our room and discovered that they had given us one bed. Liz shrieked. When she made the reservation, she had asked them for *two separate* beds in one room. We'd had so much fun on our drive there, though, that I automatically thought, *Yeah, sure you wanted two beds . . . I don't think so.* And then I proceeded to act on that assumption.

Liz was a little surprised and annoyed by my amorous advances. It turned out that she really *didn't* assume we were going to jump right into bed and get hot first thing. So I got the message pretty fast, and stayed patient.

We drank and smoked and skied for the next week straight, getting along better and better with each passing day. On the last night we had together, we finally got together in a really successful and intimate way. It was a snowy, mysterious Austrian night full of sexual anticipation. Then fulfillment.

Bliss. All night long. I'll never forget it.

By the time we said good-bye and I flew off, we were both head-over-heels in love.

Liz returned from Austria six months earlier than expected, and we moved in together. We were both pretty thrilled about it, but a bit scared. She was thirteen years younger than me, and still needed one more quarter's worth of units to graduate, which she wasn't crazy about doing. I urged her to finish, explaining that she would always regret it if she left it incomplete. So she did.

We had a volatile, but terrific relationship. The problem was she always wanted me around all the time, and I had to work. I also had these two sons that I wanted to see, so I'd ask Liz to come along to kill two birds with one stone.

Liz was pretty positive about my keeping a close relationship with the boys, so we took them everywhere with us. One very positive aspect of our early days was that Liz didn't act like a stepmom; instead she treated the boys like friendly nephews, which worked out really well. They already had a mom—there was no point trying to compete with her.

We brought them with us to Hawaii, Mexico, Spain, Tahiti, Fiji, Barbados, and other places most of every summer, thinking those trips would be good growing experiences for them. Liz spent so much time helping me raise Brett and Cameron during those years, she felt like she didn't need to have kids.

We talked a little about getting married, and I almost proposed three months after we moved in together. We were on a surfing and camping trip in Baja, just feeling really good. She knew I almost blurted it out, but I held back, letting my fear of being married again get the best of me. Cold feet!

A while after that, I told her, "Don't expect to get married any time soon. I'm just not ready to do it again."

She totally stopped mentioning marriage. I thought, *Wow, she's willing to just roll with it.*

≈

By 1997, brother Billy was living not too far from me in Laguna Beach. He was sober and had a girlfriend named Gina Mead, who had helped keep him on a pretty steady course for quite some time. Then, I'm not sure exactly what happened, but the wheels fell off the cart.

He started taking drugs again, and new, different, weird girlfriends started showing up, and weird events started happening all around him. Soon enough it was back to getting him out of jail in the middle of the night, helping him cope with his DUIs, and on and on and on. The usual.

That same year, for some reason, sooner then I'd thought, I was ready to get married.

The trauma of divorcing Kris was finally far behind me. The boys were growing up. Liz and I had been living together for almost five years. Business had its ups and downs, but I knew enough now to ride it out, be patient, and jump back in at the right moment.

I proposed to Liz up in Santa Barbara, walking along Butterfly Beach in Montecito. She cried and said, "I'm not sure if I can."

What?

From the beginning, I had told her that I didn't expect to get married again, and she had adjusted to that. So when I proposed out of the blue, it shook her—in fact, it kind of pissed her off.

It took Liz a while to adjust to my new mindset about marriage, but eventually, it got worked out. About a year later, we got married in Maui at the Makawao Union church and had a great reception at Mama's Fish House. God, what a great celebration! Way different than my first marriage.

Two uncles showed up from Oahu, Clarence and Harold, and my mom and several of her friends were there, of course. All of the families and friends had a blast.

My brother Bill wasn't there because he wouldn't come without his current psycho girlfriend. And the two of them together were so explosive that I just couldn't run the risk of having them throw a big scene. I told him not to come, sad as that was. That turned out to be a good decision, though, since the current psycho girlfriend had him arrested and jailed for domestic violence around the same time as the wedding.

Kris gradually became bitter that Liz and I were happy together, that we were married and it wasn't just a temporary thing anymore. She sued for more money a couple of times, which got pretty ugly. Eventually, Liz and Kris began to really dislike each other.

After several years of that, plus a fair share of having fun and partying, Liz and I started having trouble dealing with all of my family problems. I felt I had financial obligations to take care of my mom and my brother Billy, in addition to all the time and energy I spent rescuing, moving, and generally looking after them both. Liz came to see this as time and money taken away from us as a couple, and she resented it.

To spend more time near me, Liz became the bookkeeper in my office. When business got better and had to grow a lot, finances got more complicated. I had to get CPAs in to take care of the financial end, so Liz got kind of fired, you might say, which was awkward and uncomfortable for us both. Liz was miffed, and I felt awful.

So sure enough, at one point around 1992, we agreed to take some time off. Liz went on a one-month trip. When she came back, we huddled about our relationship and realized that we had to fish or cut bait. Luckily we both wanted to stay together, and decided to commit ourselves to the relationship.

~

One of the outcomes of this resolution was deciding to have a child. Liz's doctor thought it might take a while, but she got pregnant within a month. Then we found out it was a girl. Boom! Just like that, a new daughter, sister, granddaughter!

We named her Lockley Leilani McElroy. Lockley is Liz's mom's maiden name. Leilani is my sister's middle name. Lockley has been an absolute godsend of a child, just an awesome girl. Liz struggles sometimes with raising a child, although she has done a stellar job at it. She complains about how hard it is. We talk about it.

Liz and I have always been deeply in love, but I think our upbringing left a lot to be figured out on the fly. Her family was really strict, religious and unforgiving, and mine was pretty loose. Neither of us had great role models to emulate.

Liz had always rebelled against her parents' attempts to make her into an Ivy League student like her dad. He was from a really poor family but did so well that he made it to Princeton. Her mom was from a very wealthy family in Rochester, New York, then went to Mills College in Oakland, California. Both her parents had great hopes for her rise in society, but she never wanted to be the dutiful daughter and buckle under their way of seeing her.

Even more of a problem was that Liz's expectations of our life together seemed to me at times a little unrealistic. Since she still wanted me all to herself, it felt like I was abandoning her every time I went to the office. But I had to work. My business was heating up all the time and I was responsible for many mouths to feed.

It didn't make for a very smooth or easy relationship, especially when we were partying and drinking a lot. I think we were both feeling threatened, and we started pushing each other's buttons.

Sometimes things were really good, and sometimes they were really bad. Knock-down, drag-out shouting matches. We separated a few times, one or the other of us moving out to go on a trip overseas or visit one of the houses we owned in Hawaii or Mexico. But we always got back together after a few weeks. And we worked it out. We still get into fights now and then, but they're mild compared to what they were in the past.

Chapter Eleven

In 2000, Mom retired to Maui. By this time we were all calling her Tutu, just like the kids did. Big brother Billy moved in with her about a year or so after that. In 2002, Bill started his own heavy equipment earth-moving and road-building company, and for a while he was doing really well. But in 2005, I had to pull Bill off the island of Maui before he got himself killed.

The bad news came when the phone rang at two a.m., waking us from a deep sleep. But it was three hours earlier in Hawaii, only ten p.m. I heard a scratchy voice that I knew right away was my favorite cousin, Kama.

"Ron, get on the next plane. Please, come get your brother out of here. Fast! As soon as possible. Tutu can't handle him anymore."

I got on the plane as soon as I could, worried about what I would find. According to the report from cousin Kama, things were pretty bad. I'd seen Billy a year before, at my sister's son's wedding. Maybe I was just used to him, but Billy hadn't seemed so bad then. I hoped they were just exaggerating.

They weren't.

I landed later the same day as I got the call and rented a car. By the time I'd driven to my mom's house it was getting dark and it wasn't that easy to see clearly, since there were no street lights where she lived.

But when I pulled up and hurried into her house, I saw an old man I didn't know standing just inside the door. I'm pretty good at identifying relatives or good friends from a distance, but this guy just didn't look familiar. Then he turned and looked at me.

Damn. It was my brother.

Billy and I stared at each, reading in each other's eyes the mutual understanding of just how fucked up things were.

Bill wasn't carrying much more than 160 pounds. At six feet tall, he was a walking skeleton. Loose clothes, hunched over, withdrawn eyes, uncertain speech, premature white-gray hair, a few nervous-induced scratchy sores, unprovoked flinches, lost stares into space. . . . Other than that, Billy looked a lot like me. Always accused of being brothers growing up, we'd just laugh and say "Daaah!!" accompanied by our trademark blank stare into nowhere slightly above head level. Now things weren't so funny anymore.

I hate telling these stories but what can I say? He's my brother. It's the albatross around my neck, the truth about my life. So here's the rest of what happened.

Mom came out, and I could see that her magic had finally let her down. Age had removed the resilience that had always kept her going throughout her long and arduous life's mission of keeping Billy alive.

As soon as I walked into the house, Billy started ranting about a mumbo-jumbo conspiracy against him. I listened intently, nodding every once in a while, while he tells me about some girl who has it in for him. It's a conspiracy, he says. She's the daughter of some local crime thug. Oh yeah, and her bodyguard is some jujitsu kung fu crazy dude who's just looking for an excuse to kick someone's ass.

I've never seen my mom so relieved to see me. But I was disappointed in myself. How could I have turned a blind eye to this for so long, leaving her right in the middle of this insanity?

I know all the specialists say, "It's not your responsibility—you're enabling." Well, okay. Should I have left Billy to fend for himself in prison, being beaten to a pulp? He had already died twice, and been unmercifully brought back to his living hell.

It turned out that a whole bunch of weird shit had been swirling around my big brother as he got further and further away from reality.

Apparently, Billy had been doing some work for Laird Hamilton, the big wave surfer who's married to Gabrielle Reece. They'd hired Billy to use his earth-moving equipment to carve out a better access from their properties to the ocean, which he had accomplished with his usual finesse.

Unfortunately, they had a little dispute over what they owed him for services rendered. Billy's method of handling the issue was direct: he left his massive rig on their property, blocking access to anyone trying to get in or out of the area. Our friends Sierra and Paul, who really do love Billy, were still trying to make things right on this one.

I wasn't sure why Billy thought this was such a great tactic, especially after I heard the next story. It seems that yet another disagreement on payment had surfaced with a customer for whom he was scraping out a road. He again blocked access and refused to move, even spending the night in his tractor to make sure no one passed or tried to mess with the blockade until the proper toll was collected.

Fed up, the customer arrived on the scene with a few thugs to persuade him to understand that there had been a slight miscalculation.

Unpleasantries were exchanged, tempers boiled, one of Billy's opponents went to grab a weapon, and another ran his truck smack into Billy's big excavator. It didn't make a dent, but everyone kept trying to show everyone else who was boss. Suspecting the worst, Billy set his ominous forty-foot-long metal tracks in motion, getting close enough to whip his bucket —it was the size of a VW—just above his enemy's truck cab in one fluid, arching swoop. T-Rex jaws perched right above the occupant, who was now concerned for his life.

All combatants backed off.

I noticed pretty quick that his four-wheel-drive F-150 truck was a mess. But this wasn't the result of sabotage, it, too, was all Billy.

Late one night, during one of his flights into cerebral shutdown, he ended up driving down to the beach. He told me how he was drawn to what he described as a luminescent fish cruising just below the surface. He watched them jumping out of the water, trailing sparkling, colorful, iridescent droplets in slow motion. . . . The way he told it, it sounded like a scene from the Beatles' *Yellow*

Submarine movie. He wanted to get as close as possible to this fascinating Technicolor water world, and drove out as far as he could on the low tide–exposed sand and coral. Sure, who wouldn't?

He was gazing at this show for what seemed to him like hours . . . until he was rudely awakened by the sound of crashing waves and a painfully bright sunlit morning.

What had started out as a firm parking place was now an ocean whose high tide was at about window level. But Bill wasn't fazed. He managed to recruit some very surprised early-morning fisherman to help him tow the saltwater-logged truck back to dry land.

I couldn't stomach any more of these foolish stories and Billy's teeth-grinding excuses. I told him I was buying his ticket and we needed to get to the airport come hell or high water in no more than two days. I figured I'd better move quickly, before he came up with another *Jerry Springer* episode.

But I didn't move quickly enough.

As I was trying to figure out where to move him, Billy decided to try to get his truck in driving order—he'd worked out a trade for a recently crashed BMW 320i—and one of his crack-head girlfriends was helping him with a transmission problem on the truck.

Can you picture this?

Billy was lying on his back under the truck, with one hand holding a massive wrench. The girl was behind the wheel. Billy yelled at her to "edge forward slowly." But her brain heard these instructions as *Go backwards as fast as you can!*

Miraculously, the extent of Billy's damage was a broken wrist and some scrapes and bruises. Sadly, the girl was unable to withstand the meth bugs crawling just below surface of her skin. I heard later that, about a month after this mishap, she inexplicably leaped from the back of a speeding truck and died. Billy always had a fatal attraction for these types of girlfriends.

It was clear that we had to get him out of here. I set to work putting Billy's part of Tutu's house back together so Mom wouldn't have to deal with it.

Billy's mess reflected just how crazy he'd gotten. It took me the entire day to clean out, haul away, and reorganize the garage where he'd stored his stuff, literally hosing everything down just before dark on my first full day in Maui. Next—I can't believe I did this—I cleaned my brother's room. But it wasn't like making the bed and putting some clothes in a hamper. It was a nightmare. I had to haul out all of his assorted crap, and all the furniture except the bed. Took down the blankets and towels covering the windows, and scrubbed the whole room clean after removing all the trash. After a half day's work, it looked relatively normal.

And the whole time, Billy was useless, helpless, but never still. He was constantly walking through and around stuff, rubbing his chin, murmuring inaudibly.

Mom was already starting to feel sorry for Billy. I had to take this decision out of her hands, and quickly. Where could he go?

Molokai might work, but I knew that in about a week I'd be getting two a.m. calls from angry relatives to get him the hell off the island. Mainland Mexico was out of the question. I could just image what Billy would do with the drug cartels.

I was developing some real estate in San Juanico, in Baja, and if he could keep his brain in some sort of working order, his earth-moving skills could definitely come in handy. My friend Jamie was helping me out down there, and he liked Billy. That sounded like the best plan.

I called Liz to explain, and she tried to talk me out of it. But what did she want me to do? I really didn't see where we had many choices. Finally, she realized it was futile and gave up.

So it's a thumbs-up. Operation Billy is ready to go. A few days after, I get Billy on the plane and we fly back to California.

Chapter Twelve

We're heading down to San Juanico, in southern Baja. which would be both far away and also give Billy a job he could do, coming up with ways to improve the property construction site.

I recruited my younger son, Cameron, who was then eighteen, to make the drive with Bill and me, so we could switch off and make better time. He loved driving through Baja and he loved hanging out with his Uncle Bill. That's the sad thing: Billy was actually loved by a lot of people, especially my kids and all their buddies. Maybe it was because he was such a big kid himself.

Cameron was pretty mature for his age. He'd already traveled a good portion of the globe on family trips, and he'd had to absorb his parents' divorce at an early age. Quick and sharp-witted, he's rarely short of words or opinions, and he's vehemently loyal to loved ones, including his Uncle Bill.

I had seen a clear example of his loyalty to family and friends when he was fourteen. We had a bit of quiet time together while driving one day, and I seized the opportunity to question an area of concern.

"Cam, you know I enjoy all of your friends, and I think they're all solid kids, but there's one kid I'm concerned about: Skylar. Love 'im to death, but I sense that he's stoned, smells like alcohol a bit too often, and on top of that he's not going to school. I don't want him to be a negative influence on you. I'm not telling you who to hang out with, but it is a concern of mine."

"I hear what you're saying, Dad. But the way I see it, I'm the stronger person, and I think that I'll be the positive influence on his life versus the other way around."

Cam's response rendered me speechless but contented. What a smart kid. I was a lucky dad, and as far as I was concerned, enough said.

Thankfully, everything was pretty uneventful during our twenty-hour haul on the sole two-lane road through Baja. Cameron and I switched off about every four or five hours; Billy pretty much slept the entire trip. Occasionally, he'd wake up and make some harebrained comment, which was great comic relief on our long monotonous drive.

"Oh dude, you see those circles out there in the ocean?" Billy pointed towards a half-dozen fifty-meter-wide rings made of rope and floats, some sort of fishery equipment. "Those are the same receptacles they use in Hawaii."

"What?"

"Yeah," he said, excited to share this information. "Aliens travel through those circles when they land in the ocean. They're the entry gates to their encampments."

"Encampments?"

"Yeah, they live inside the base of volcanoes, and those circles are the ends of these long wormholes that allow them to go back and forth."

"Cool, Billy. Go back to sleep."

One thing I have observed with icers: The further they get from their last brain-melt, the more they display progressively longer periods of comalike sleep, interrupted by voracious appetite. This is the flip side of long periods abstaining from sleep and food while the meth is searing their brain like a fresh piece of ahi.

Along with these long periods of comalike sleep separated by ravenous hunger, Billy's brain seemed unable to hold one thought at a time. I watched when we stopped to stretch our legs and my brother walked over to something, picked it up, carried it to another location, dropped it, picked something else up . . . repeating the exercise endlessly. Upon reaching each pit stop (for gas, restroom, snacks), Cam and I would get some sad comic relief from our long arduous drive by watching Uncle Bill for as long as we could handle it. Unfortunately, it reminded me of our dad's backward walking and burying money in the desert years ago.

Worse, wherever we went, people thought Bill was my dad. It was embarrassing, sad, and painful. What could I say? "Oh, he's not my dad. He's just my brother the meth head. Hasn't aged as well."

I hate to make light of Billy's drug addiction and addled brain, but I'm allowed to. I'm his brother and I'm taking care of his ass.

The last three to four hours' drive was over dirt, dunes, ravines, mountains, and salt flats, the infamous North

Road, where unwary travelers have gotten lost even during daylight crossings, literally for days.

I'd made a mistake on this road a couple of years back that burned some cautious respect into my psyche and made every decision after that a careful calculation. Back then, I'd made a U-turn on a muddy salt flat lower down, figuring I could find a better route if I went higher. But this brought me to a spot that was far worse than simply digging through stinky mud. This North Road was heavily patrolled with military checkpoints—out in the middle of nowhere. I suddenly found myself in the middle of six .30 caliber machine gun–mounted Humvees manned by a unit of fully armed soldiers with seemingly nothing to shoot at except piles of shucked clam shells from several small, dusty fishing villages. I wasn't sure if they were trying to stop the transport of drugs or accommodate it. I just kept my eyes on the road and sped away as fast as I could. Lesson learned!

On this trip with Cameron and Billy, however, it was all peaceful and good. We took Billy to San Juanico, where he could work under the supervision of my good friend Jamie. I knew that my brother had the skills to do what was needed down there—if he could just hold it together.

"Do a good job, bro," I said.

Bill assured me, of course, that he could and would.

But once again, it turned out to be too good to be true.

Back at home, I was busy, as usual. I had a whole lot going on with one business deal or another, plus looking after the rest of my family. So it was about six months before

I was able to get back down to Baja to check on Bill and see what was up.

I'd heard a few rumblings, but it didn't sound too bad. That's because the reports from Baja were sugarcoated by Jamie and other friends who were trying not to burden me. Reading between the lines, though, I realized that I'd better make the time to fly down and check it out myself.

I was in a hurry, so instead of driving, this time I flew into La Paz. That's not the closest town you can fly into, but it is a big city by Mexican standards and has all the big-box stores—good for stocking up on supplies. I zipped through customs, only to be left stranded for another twenty minutes in the dry desert heat of the pickup zone outside the terminal, waiting for my brother to pick me up and getting madder by the second.

Then I saw him coming.

Right away, I saw why he was late: he was driving one of my good company trucks, but it was so beat up, he was limping down the road at no more than twenty miles an hour. The huge white Ford F-250 four-door 4x4 V-10, capable of carrying or towing massive loads, looked like a wartorn amphibious assault vehicle that had clearly lost a battle.

The shock of seeing that sad truck idle up to the curb left me speechless. Billy gave me a dopey, sheepish greeting, and started right off on some useless explanation of why he was late.

I got in the truck, shaking my head.

Billy kept talking. He and I have never gotten into a serious fight, but right about then I wanted nothing more than to sink my fist into his excuse-filled mouth so he would just stop talking.

Instead, I asked, "What the fuck is wrong with you?"

He just kept fumbling through excuses, a telltale sign of someone who is hard up for a quick fix.

I picked up his cigarette lighter from the dashboard and looked at it. Sure enough, there was a heavy pastelike residue seared into the coil, rendering it useless. Smoking crack is nowhere near the jolt that smoking ice is, but it's about the closest you can get out here in the desert. Judging by the layers of residue, Bill must have been smoking a whole lot in this truck while speeding around, out of his mind, crashing into whatever was so unfortunate as to be in his path.

Later that day, I talked to Jamie. Calmly, unemotionally, he laid out what had been going on over the last few months. Sounded a lot like what had happened in Maui. The bottom line was that San Juanico was no longer a place that could tolerate Billy. In fact, he was in major danger of getting killed if he stayed.

Once again, my big brother had found the assholes, and they had found him. Jamie told me that Billy was ground zero in the middle of a turf dispute between two San Diego surfers, each claiming to have more rights than the other at one of their home surf breaks. Apparently, Billy just happened to be on the spot when the thugs decided to exert a show of local claim by smacking Bill's latest unsuspecting best friend over the head with a two-by-four.

Billy responded with his usual lack of discretion, doing severe harm to his opponent's face and body with a vicious claw tire iron.

Typically, in scraps like these, both sides eventually move on. But not these particular individuals. They made it clear to Jamie that Billy was going to be a dead man if he wasn't gone from San Juanico within seventy-two hours.

I looked at my watch. That was about seventy-two hours ago.

Later that same day, Billy and I were both on plane back to Southern California.

I don't want to give you the impression that big brother Bill's life has been nonstop insanity. There was at least one stretch of sobriety—seven years—that long-term relationship with his fiancée, Gina Mead. Billy had even stopped smoking cigarettes, since that was really important to Gina. It's just that Billy's life is like a big Hawaiian wave—what goes up must come crashing down.

Billy and Gina had been going out for a year and a half. It was the most recent step in what I hoped would be Billy's creating a lifestyle that would be healthy, positive, and predictable.

But then, the inevitable: Billy called me to say he and Gina had broken up and I should meet him at the usual spot on the beach. When I got there, he was sitting on the back of a bench taking huge tokes on a cigarette. I was sorry to see it; I knew he hadn't smoked for a year. "Hey howzit, brodoooh?"

Big handshakes and smiles all around. At that point, Billy has been leading a productive life, and it's evident from his confident demeanor. But as he starts telling me about Gina, I can't help but think, *I hope this isn't the beginning of the end, again.*

"So why did you and Gina break up?" I ask. "I thought that was going so well."

"Ah, dude, just can't do it man! No way! It wasn't my fault, I swear to God."

"Bro—no one is saying it's your fault. Maybe you just need to step back, take a couple big deep breaths."

"Yeah, maybe so. But let me tell you what was the straw that finally broke my back. You know we're doing this remodel on the house, right?"

"So?"

"Well, I just had this new white carpet installed in the family room, and Gina steps in a pile of my dog's crap—huge Rottweiler piles!—and walks right over the carpet. Well, she starts freaking out, man, I mean, really freaking out: 'What's wrong with you? Why didn't you pick it up before I stepped in it?'

"Fuck, I didn't even get a chance to explain that I was trying to finish installing the carpet before I got to the dog crap, just *Pow, you're a big freaking ass.*

"So I grab a bucket of water and sponges and start cleaning, and she's helping, but she's still just, *Wah, wah, wah . . . It's your fault . . wah, wah, wah.*

"Dude, I couldn't take it any longer. I just dumped that bucket of shitty water all over her head."

"What!? "

"Yeah, she went absolutely nuts, arms flailing, shaking her head back and forth and screaming . . . just crazy!"

"Oh my god, dude! So, what happened then?"

"You won't believe it, bra. She said, 'It's time to shit or get off the pot.' She made me go to a preacher with her, you know, come-to-Jesus time."

"The shitty water made her want to get married sooner?"

Billy laughed. "Yeah, guess so. So I went. I listen to the preacher preach about commitment and love and trust and faith, and I'm like, *Yeah, it's probably good to live with all these cool ideas.*"

Wow, I was thinking, *Billy really is mellowing out in his later years.*

Of course, the story's not over yet.

"Anyways, I'm walking out of the church thinking, *Damn should we get married? If I only had a strong sign that this was the right thing to do, it would be a whole lot easier.* Then—I shit you not—a huge seagull flying overhead dropped the biggest green, white, and black shit right on top of my head!"

We both start laughing so hard that our sides are aching.

"*Fautor per filiolus,* bro," says Billy. "Favored by the gods." I know he's quoting the McElroy family coat of arms—yes, we have one, and Billy's into that stuff.

"So that was it?"

Billy nods his head. "May as well pack up and move to Maui," he says.

Well, it was downhill from there, as you already know.

But things, as they always seem to do, started looking up after that. Billy and his son, Brandon, from an earlier relationship with a woman named Angela, finally moved in with Tutu. Brandon's mother was having tough times and asked if Billy would take him, and that was it. Tutu's all about family, so Bill and Brandon, now eight, moved back to Maui, and Bill began finding the occasional job as a seasoned operator-engineer.

As for my relationship with Bill today, I keep wondering: Is it worth it to keep patching up something that clearly can't be permanently fixed? Who am I trying to please? What is the nature of my obligation? These questions surely deserve to be answered, but there are no easy answers. Most of my friends and relatives don't think so.

For me, it always seems to come down to the same thing. We're family. You don't abandon your brother, no matter what—you just provide a helping hand when one is needed. If it fixes the problem, then great, and if it doesn't—well, that's fine too.

So when people ask me why I keep helping Billy out of one jam after another, with no real progress to show for it, I can only shrug and say, "He's my brother. I can't *not* help."

Chapter Thirteen

One of the reasons I wrote this book is to figure out what my place should or shouldn't be in my brother Billy's life. I've been trying to figure that out since we were teenagers, when I began to see him clearly for the damaged soul he is and stopped believing he was an ideal role model for me to emulate.

Unfortunately, Billy's not the only big problem in my family.

As you know, my sister Susie hasn't been in our lives much over the years. When her two boys got old enough they left, and one got married a couple of years ago. The boys and their father sued the Tony and Susan Alamo Foundation for damages and won, as have others. But Susie still remains inside the cult. We thought for sure she would leave when the suits were successful and Tony ended up in jail, but she didn't. She's still loyal to her adopted family, regardless of her bonds of marriage or children.

How did Susan turn out this way? Why was Bill like he was? How come I've been able to lead a relatively normal, productive life? We were all three of us children of the same parents, growing up in the same family. What went wrong? What went right?

I have no idea really. But my mom is right with all of her Hawaiian superstition and magical thinking. Life is sure mysterious. And messy.

∾

Meanwhile, my kids are doing fine. The deep-seated insecurity and paranoia that persistently plagued me and my siblings seem to be in remission in the next generation.

Lockley is in second grade now and loves school. The boys both have graduated from college—Brett from San Diego State one year ago, and Cameron from UCSB just three months ago. Cameron's off travelling in Indonesia, and Brett lives in Maui, working as a kite-surfing instructor. They are great, great kids: respectful, competent and smart. I am truly blessed.

My marriage is good too. We both want to get divorced every other week, but that would be a terrible idea and the moment passes. So instead, we enjoy making up. We work hard at trying to be stable and conscious of how good our lives really are. We try to keep reminding ourselves that we have phenomenal good fortune and to be grateful!

As for me, I don't think I'm the sharpest tool in the shed, I just think I know how to make things work. I just like the challenge and stimulation of getting things done.

When I started my company, REMC, I was in the middle of a divorce and pretty down and out, with big alimony and child-support payments to make each month. But that didn't stop me. I got a bank to give me a $50,000 business loan and I was off and running!

After about fifteen years, it seemed we were closing in on the peak of our upward market cycle, so I decided it was the right time to sell and cash out.

I was able to orchestrate a bidding match among three of my biggest competitors, which culminated in one of the highest multiples per net revenue in our industry. But then, the winning bidder, a group from New York, Broadway Partners, tried to pull the well known "New York close" in the eleventh hour. My brilliant longtime good friend, Eric Larson, warned me it would happen.

As he predicted, they tried to give us a haircut the day the deal was supposed to close. They said basically, *Either take a reduction in price or we're going to take our ball and go home.* Well, my only saving grace was I had made them put down a deposit of $200,000 when we originally negotiated the deal—not very common in the world of buying and selling companies. It still would have been painful to walk away from six months of due diligence work with a legal and accounting bill in excess of $300,000 at that point, but I was willing to take that chance.

We were all on a conference call that Friday morning with their company bigwigs, their high-powered attorneys making up reasons why they needed to cut the price . . . on and on and on. Finally, I just told them to stick it—truly, just shove it!—and hung up the phone. I killed the biggest pay day I had ever contemplated in my life. Oh well.

Everybody was shocked, even my own guys. My attorney, Mark Conley, and my accountant David Larson, an old, good friend from UCSB drinking days, both thought I might want to try and meet them halfway. No, bullshit! I felt like if we gave in then they wouldn't stop; they would just keep dragging it out and chipping away. Plus, the market was starting to fall over its peak! So I left that day and went home to my wife with the bad news. She was disappointed as well, as you might imagine.

But Liz had already organized a trip down to San Diego to spend the weekend with Brett and his girlfriend, so we left town. I turned off my phone and computer and we went to drown our sorrows.

Late Sunday, as we're all going to dinner, I finally turn on my phone. Mark had been trying to get me all weekend.

"Ron, I've been calling you since Friday night. These guys want to make this deal. They want to meet you halfway!"

"Tell them to stick it again."

A few minutes later he calls back, even more breathless.

"Ron this time they say they're going to sue your ass and tie you up in court for years."

Mark's a sharp guy. He'd told them that he wasn't even going to tell me that they said that, because he knew the deal would really be over. So we decided to have Mark go back and tell them that the other buyer had been calling, but because of our tentative agreement we hadn't talked to them, yet. Mark also told them to sue me or do whatever they wanted but, bottom line, *if every bit of the original purchase price wasn't wired to my bank by nine o'clock Monday morning, the deal was history.*

Monday was a good morning! They did it. I got exactly what I wanted, the original high price, signed, sealed, and delivered.

I was proud of myself, but I felt very fortunate to be able to see the big picture. So much of business is psychological. I approach every deal with the whole psychology of the players all mapped out in my head. Like a conductor seeing how to make music flow or a writer developing a plot, I try to see what has to happen to make a deal work.

I also love to work with really sharp people. It has become the favorite part of work for me.

And that's how I've been able to make it in real estate. I saw where there was a vacuum, a need for vacation rental properties in great places where nothing much had been developed yet. So I began building vacation rental properties in Maui, then Baja, and now finally in Zihuatanejo, Mexico.

The two properties in Maui were on land I had bought during the downturn in the market, when the Japanese exodus took place in the mid-1990s. I built a couple of modest structures that were very popular with vacation renters on the North Shore, by Paia, where Willie Nelson hangs out. They did well, but then I sold them when the market was at its peak.

Then, in Baja, I bought a piece of desert on a surf break known as Scorpion Bay. I built a little storage bungalow and had lots of glorified camping nights with friends and family. Liz didn't like the desert environment much, though, so I sold it. Again, I bought low and sold high, and got almost ten times what I had paid for it.

For some reason, real estate has always made sense to me. I've spent the last four years building a project known as Playa Loma Bonita, an authentic Mexican retreat. We encountered problem after problem not too long after buying the property. But you have to look long term and know that things will correct themselves eventually, right? First there was a rash of shark attacks—mostly an hour-and-a-half drive away, but still not what most potential buyers want to hear about being nearby. Then there was an attack of swine flu. Major hysteria persuaded millions of potential visitors that if you so much as stepped foot in Mexico you'd get sick and die in days.

Then the Playa Loma Bonita project was hurt by a lack of confidence and extreme risk-aversion by folks worried about the crumbling American economy. Then the world economy. And then forty-three thousand people killed in the Mexican drug wars since 2006, the majority of that in the last couple of years. Hmmm. Well . . .

We postponed further construction for a while, but finally opened up in November 2011. We've also done lots of community work—building roads and schools, fixing structures, bringing electricity to the area in an effort to develop a good bond with the community. It worked for a while, but now the cartels are just infiltrating everything. Until the extortion settles down, it looks like we won't be building anything else for a while.

My feeling is that everything comes in cycles, and this drug plague violence will cycle out too, just as it has in Colombia.

In January 2011, I relaunched my shared office business, Realofficecenters.com, after removing my noncompete clause from the sale of the previous company. We are growing fast and hard. Our plan is to expand with a shared office location presence throughout the Southern California office market while the market is soft—"soft" meaning favoring office tenants like myself securing long-term commitments on large chunks of space. We build it out, wire it up, furnish and staff it, and then rent it out to people who don't want to have their own long term inflexible office lease. It's an easy, quick solution to a beautiful and presentable workplace as and when it's needed.

≈

Every aspect of my life has been touched by Bill—family, friends, finances, emotions, adventures, trouble, heartache, fun, trauma, or just craziness. One way or another, life goes on. Maybe it's just the natural way. I remember one time when I was a kid, I accidentally stepped on part of an anthill, leaving a good portion of the tiny creatures dead or injured, scattered, and in disarray. But soon the ones that were still capable of moving were joined by reinforcements from below, back on task within minutes. I wondered, *How can all this carnage take place and in the matter of a few blinks it's business as usual*?

That's my life with Billy. Maybe that's just life.

I love reconnecting with my brother, even if he seems to have spent his downtime conducting field study for a book he's working on: *101 Ways to Destroy Yourself*. Whenever I see him, there's always goofy smiles and a "What up, bro?" followed by a big embrace.

More often than not, he's fresh off an airplane or thirty-hour bus ride, lugging an Army-issue duffle with all his worldly possessions, Billy can't wait to help me out with my pressing business issues.

"Alriiiiiight brodooooh!!! Let's get to it . . . Where is this cracker and all his tractors?"

I relish the thought that I still have a living brother. Physical, mental, emotional, psychological, and chemical—every thinkable form of abuse has been inflicted or self-inflicted on his spirit, mind, and body . . . and yet here he is, smiling like it's just another day in paradise.

I have a deep, genuinely good feeling inside when I think about Billy doing well. The same smile I get when he says something completely off the wall.

The patience I've gained from trying to cope and understand his point of view has been instrumental in teaching me to temper my once-rigid expectations about raising two sons. The ability to find comic relief when everyone and everything around you has become so damned serious and important is Billy's gift, and I treasure it.

Books to Read

Ku Kanaka: Stand Tall: A Search for Hawaiian Values
  by George Hu'eu Sanford Kanahele
  University of Hawaii Press 1986

Legends and Myths of Hawaii: The Fables and Folk-Lore of a Strange People
  by His Haweaiian Majesty King David Kalakua
  Mutual Pub Co 1990

Hawaii's Story
  by Hawaii's Queen Liliuokalani
  Mutual Publishing 1991

The Betrayal of Liliuokalani: Last Queen of Hawaii 1838-1917
  Mutual Publishing 1991

The Curse of Lono
  By Hunter S. Thompson, Illustrated by Ralph Steadman
  Taschen 2005

Aloha America: Hula Circuits through the U.S. Empire
  By Andria L. Imada
  Duke University Press 2012

Lost Kingdom: Hawaii's Last Queen, the Sugar Kings and America's First Imperial Adventure
    by Julia Flynn Siler
    Atlantic Monthly Press 2012

Films to See

Blue Hawaii. Elvis Presley, 1961, with Angela Landsburyas and Hawaiin favorite Hilo Hattie.

Paradise, Hawaiian Style. The 1996 movie also starring Elvis Presley with James Shigetsu and Donna Butterworth.

Endless Summer. Bruce Brown classic surf documentary released in 1966.

Endless Summer Two. Updated 30 years later.

From Here to Eternity. The 1953 film directed by Fred Zinnemanm starring Burt Lancaster, Deborah Kerr, Frank Sinatra, Ernest Borgnine, about 1941 attack on Pearl Harbor.

Hawaii. The 1966 film directed by George Roy Hill staring Max Von Sydow, Julie Andrews and Jocelyne LaGarde. Based on the novel by James Michener.

The Hawaiians. The 1970 film also based on the book by Michener, starring Charleton Heston, Geraldine Chaplin and Tina Chen.

Heart of the Sea. A one hour PBS documentary about the legendary female surfer Reil "Kapolioka'ehuka" Sun directed by Lisa Denker and Charlotte LaGarde.

Picture Bride. A 1994 Japanese movie starring Youki Kudoh as an 18 year old Japanese mail-order bride who comes to Hawaii to marry a man much older than she and work as a farm laborer in the sugar cane fields.

Hawaii Five-0. A TV show that ran for 12 seasons from 1968-1980, starring Jack Lord, James McArthur, Kam Fong and Zulu, filmed in Oahu, to Waikiki to Makapuu Point.

The Descendants. The 2011 American comedy-drama film directed by Alexander Payne, based on the novel by Kaui Hart Hemings, starring George Clooney, Shailene Woodley, Judy Greet, Matthew Lillard and Beau Bridges. Clooney plays a man who ultimately comes to understand what happens to the beauty and culture of indigenous Hawaii when wealthy outsiders develop Islands, and then does the right thing.

About the Author

Ron McElroy is the third and youngest child of William and Arlene McElroy. His late father William was of mixed German and Scottish descent and his mother Arlene, called "Tutu", is an indigenous Hawaiian who grew up on the islands and was the greatest influence in his cultural and ethnic identity. Ron was born into poverty in Southern California where he survived discrimination, police violence and an abusive, mentally unbalanced father.

Street smart and reckless, McElroy got into trouble at school but did well in athletics and quickly realized he couldn't follow in the footsteps of his self-destructive older brother Bill. He attended community college and then graduated from the University of California at Santa Barbara. Spending summers with his mother's family in Hawaii, Ron also learned to surf and became a high-ranking amateur surfer.

After college, Ron sold surfing goods for his sponsors. Then Ron finally discovered his true calling: real estate. He worked for others and gradually became an entrepreneur with his own companies in the shared office industry plus vacation residence and rentals in Mexico and Hawaii.

Ron and his wife Elisabeth live in Laguna Beach, California. He has three children, sons Brett and Cameron, and daughter Lockley. All three kids have been high achievers academically but most importantly show a genuine respect and generosity towards others. He says "After almost thirty years of working, raising kids, and living life to its absolute fullest, I'm still plagued with thoughts of not doing enough. So I've written this book!"

The result is both a personal memoir and a unique look at the cultural, political, and social issues of indigenous Hawaiians on the islands and the mainland.

Made in the USA
Las Vegas, NV
22 October 2020